ALL IN GOOD FAITH

A Resource Book
For
Multi-faith Prayer

Edited by:

Jean Potter
Marcus Braybrooke

Published by

The World Congress of Faiths

All in Good Faith

First published in 1997 in Great Britain by

The World Congress of Faiths,
2 Market Street,
Oxford OX1 3EF

ISBN 0 905468 01 5

British Library Cataloguing in Publication Data
A catalogue record for this book is available from the British Library

All in good faith : a resource book for multi-faith prayer
1. Prayers 2. Prayer 3. Interfaith worship
I. Potter, Jean II. Braybrooke, Marcus
291.4'3

Printed and bound by Quorn Litho,
62 Queens Road, Loughborough, Leicestershire LE11 1HH

ALL IN GOOD FAITH

A Resource Book for Multi-faith Prayer

CONTENTS

Sir Alan Richmond

1919 - 1997

Alan Richmond, who was himself heir to two religious traditions, was a generous and enthusiastic supporter of efforts to increase friendship and co-operation between people of different faiths.

Alan was born in Katowice, which was then in Germany, on October 12th, 1919. When he was a year old, his parents moved to Berlin, where Alan grew up and was educated. His family were Jewish. Although they were not Orthodox, they observed the Sabbaths and the High Holy Days. Alan attended Hebrew classes and took his bar-mitzvah. After study in Switzerland he came to Britain just before the Second World War. Meanwhile his parents and sister made their escape from the Nazis to Brazil and from there to the USA. It was not until after the war that Alan met up with his family again, although he had by then begun his career in Britain and decided to make that country his home.

In Britain Alan took various jobs in the Engineering Industry, whilst also studying, on a part-time basis, for engineering qualifications, including his Ph.D., which he was awarded in 1954. He devoted himself for 35 years to Further and Higher Education. In 1953, he became Head of the Engineering Department at the Welsh College of Advanced Technology, Cardiff. In 1959, he became Director of Lanchester College of Technology, which is now Coventry University. In 1962, because of his enthusiastic support for the idea of tertiary colleges and because he wanted to return to actual teaching, he moved to Street in Somerset and became Principal of Strode College.

Alan was knighted in 1969 for his services to education, which included voluntary service on various boards and committees. He wrote two books on problems in thermodynamics for engineering students.

Alan loved teaching and was greatly concerned for his students - devoted to their welfare both in face-to-face teaching and in evolving policies for the development of the institutions of which he was head.

After he retired from Strode College, Alan moved to Bath, where he embarked on a third career as an Industrial Arbitrator and as an examiner for the Chartered Institute of Arbitrators, work which he found of absorbing interest. He also continued as a consultant about the testing of appliances and tools and on energy conservation and air conditioning.

In July 1951, Alan married Sally. Sally, whilst also pursuing her own interests, was a constant support and inspiration to him. In time, he came to appreciate ever more deeply Sally's Christian faith. It was when I was Minister of Christ Church, Bath and Director of the Council of Christians and Jews that Mary and I got to know Alan and Sally. Alan was glad to learn of the new approach to Judaism of a growing number of Christian theologians, who stress that Jesus was a faithful Jew. He welcomed the efforts of the Churches both to rid themselves of anti-Jewish teaching and to develop a more positive and friendly relationship with the Jewish world. Alan often came with Sally to services at Christ Church and was a great support to me in my ministry there. Mary and I treasure the memory of his friendship and wise and understanding counsel.

Alan had a deep trust in God and a concern for ethical values, which he expressed in his own life. Alan actively welcomed efforts to build friendship and co-operation between members of the world religions. He was a generous supporter of the World Congress of Faiths and the International Interfaith Centre at Oxford.

Alan would have appreciated this book, which is dedicated to his memory. It has been lovingly typed by Sally. Its publication has been made possible by generous donations by his sister Gaby and by Professor and Mrs Eberhard Weddell.

> *The righteous will be remembered for ever; the memory of the*
> *righteous is a blessing".*
> *(Psalm 112,6; Proverbs 10;7)*

Marcus Braybrooke

1. INTRODUCTION

Marcus Braybrooke
Jean Potter

Occasions when people of different faiths come together to pray raise both theoretical and practical questions. The questions are not themselves new, but they are today asked more frequently as it becomes more common for people of different religions to join together in prayer.

Twenty five years ago, the World Congress of Faiths set up a small working group to consider the issues which arise when people of different faiths pray together. WCF had been a pioneer of 'All Faiths Services'. At the time, there was disquiet amongst some Christians about such services. The membership of the group therefore was confined to Christians and the discussion was, in effect, addressed to fellow Christians, although members of other faiths were consulted and some of their views were recorded.

In the subsequent twenty five years there has been a great increase in the number and variety of occasions on which people of different faiths come together to pray. Sometimes such prayers are part of big public events. For twenty years, Commonwealth Day has been marked in Britain by an observance at Westminster Abbey in which representatives of all faiths take part and which is normally attended by the Queen. At the opening of the new Parliament buildings in Canberra, Australia, prayers were offered by members of different faiths. In South Africa, the National Peace Convention which paved the way for democracy was opened in prayer by representatives from four religious traditions. This was the first time that such interreligious prayer had happened at an official state-sponsored event in South Africa. In San Francisco in 1995, to commemorate the fiftieth anniversary of the signing of the UN Charter an interfaith service was held in Grace Cathedral. Some of the services held in tribute to Diana, Princess of Wales, were interfaith in character. It is likely that the Millennium will be the occasion for many interreligious services.

On many occasions, people of various faiths have come together to pray for peace, particularly during the Gulf War, or for prisoners, or to voice their concern for the environment, as, for example, at the World Religions' Vigil during the 'Earth Summit' of United Nations Environment and Development Conference in Rio in 1992. Services related to the work of voluntary organizations are now likely to be interfaith in character (1). During or at the end of a multifaith dialogue weekend, the members of the conference may wish to share in readings from the world's scriptures and in prayers. For many years a feature of the World Congress of Faiths Annual Conference was a concluding All faiths service.

In many parts of the world, perhaps especially in India, Britain and North America, there are now local interfaith groups or councils. Many of these arrange at least an annual occasion when people of different faiths read from their scriptures or offer prayers. There was a marked increase in such occasions during the 1993 Year of Inter-religious Understanding and Co-operation.

As there is more mingling in society between people of different faiths, so the ceremonies that mark the rites of passage may become interfaith occasions. Two people who belong to different religions may decide to marry and want a ceremony that includes elements of both of their religions. At a funeral, the friends who come to pay their last respects may belong to more than one religion. Such occasions are not discussed in detail in this book.

Assemblies for worship in schools, which also raise particular questions, some of which relate to the law, are another subject not here discussed. Some of the theological and philosophical questions, however, about the relation of religions to each other and the appropriateness of praying together are the same in both ceremonies to mark rites of passage and in School Assemblies. Some of the material reproduced in this book may also be appropriate to both situations.

Praying Together

The increase in interfaith prayer has been accompanied by continuing discussion and controversy. Most of the published material to which we have had access, certainly in Britain, has been by Christians and has reflected the intra-Christian debate on this subject. This is not surprising in view of Christianity's majority status in Britain and because, compared for example to Hinduism, Christianity is traditionally exclusive in character. In preparation for this book, material has been received from India, the USA and some other countries and reference is made to this.

The intention of this book is that it should be multifaith in character, although both of us, who have edited the material, are Christians. Members of different faiths have been asked to share their views of interfaith prayer, in the context of their religion's understanding of prayer or worship or meditation.

The texts included in the anthology have also been chosen by members of the different religious communities.   This explains the unevenness in style.   In many cases the quotations are English translations from another language.   There are those for whom it is usual to address God as 'Thou', others who prefer 'You'.   Some people insist upon 'inclusive' language, whereas others are used to 'mankind' rather than 'humankind'.

There are other questions of language.   Some people speak of 'All Faiths Services', some of 'Multi-faith Observances' or of 'Interfaith Prayer'.   Some people spell inter faith as two words, some as one and some use a hyphen.   Some people avoid the word 'Worship' or 'Service' and perhaps prefer 'celebration' or 'observance'.   Again, we have not imposed editorial consistency.   There are different shades of meaning in the various terms and it would be wrong to disguise this and to mask the variety of viewpoints reflected in the terms people choose to employ.   Some names, however, are chosen to avoid offence rather than on philosophic or theological grounds.   The Westminster Abbey Commonwealth Day 'event' is called an 'observance' although it includes hymns of praise to God, sung by the whole congregation, and so would normally be considered worship.

The book is in four sections.   The first section gives some history of the development of interfaith services and of the discussion about them.   It then highlights the key issues.   There follows a series of chapters in which members of different faiths explain a little about their religions's view of prayer or worship or meditation and explain the attitude of members of that religion to interfaith prayer.   In several religions there are, not surprisingly, differences of view and each writer offers his or her personal contributions from his own her own perspective. Not all traditions could be represented.   There is no contribution, for example, from Confucianism, Shintoism or Native Spiritual traditions, although some members of all these religions have shared in prayer with members of other faiths.   There is then an article on practical matters, based on answers to a questionnaire, which was sent to many people who have arranged interfaith services.

The second part of the book is an anthology.   Twelve themes which are often used for interfaith services have been chosen and several members of different faiths have been invited to suggest suitable passages.   This section should be useful to those arranging interfaith services.   They may not have copies of all the scriptures available.   Here they will find appropriate quotations. The individual reader will also find a rich devotional resource in this section.

The third part of the book reproduces some orders of service including a beautiful 'imaginary' service by Claire Dalley, a student at Westminster College, Oxford. Each service is, of course, particular to the occasion for which it was arranged. They are not to be slavishly imitated, but may suggest new possibilities or illustrate some of the practical ways in which theoretical questions have been addressed.

The fourth part includes an annotated bibliography of collections of readings and prayers.
We are grateful to the Executive Committee of the World Congress of Faiths for inviting us to undertake this project. We are also grateful to the contributors, and to many other people who helped with this project, whose names are listed at the back, who either answered the questionnaire or who sent us sample services or who offered advice verbally or in writing. We owe a particular debt of gratitude to Sally Richmond who with loving care prepared the material for the printer. The book is dedicated to the memory of her husband Sir Alan Richmond, who was a strong and generous supporter of interfaith understanding and co-operation. Beyond that we acknowledge all who in their prayers affirm the unity of the human family. May this volume help others to learn from them.

July 1997

2. THE DEVELOPMENT OF INTERFAITH SERVICES

and

A HISTORY OF THE DISCUSSION ABOUT THEM

Marcus Braybrooke

Beginnings

The beginning of modern interfaith activity is usually dated to the World's Parliament of Religions, which was held in Chicago in 1893. It was there too that the first recorded 'act of common worship' took place. Members of different religions have, of course, interacted in various ways for centuries and perhaps on occasion prayed together.

The common worship at Chicago in 1893 was a spontaneous occurrence at the opening ceremony of the Parliament. The organist was playing the tune of the One Hundredth Psalm, when the crowd, most of whom were Christian, started to sing the familiar words. Following this, 'the hearts and voices of the multitude were led by Cardinal Gibbons in the Lord's Prayer' (1).

During the Parliament, several devotional meetings, which included readings and prayers from many religions, were held early in the morning. At the final session, after President Bonney's closing address, 'the great assembly joined with Rabbi Dr Emil G Hirsch in the Lord's Prayer. This was followed by a prayer of benediction delivered with great earnestness by Bishop Keane' (2)

Well before the 1893 World's Parliament of Religions at Chicago, leaders of the Brahmo Samaj - a Hindu reform movement dating from the early nineteenth century - had added readings from the scriptures of the world to the reading of Hindu texts. In the Theosophical movement, passages from all the scriptures were treasured.

In the early part of the twentieth century, some Christian missionary colleges in India, in order to make it easier for their Hindu and Muslim students to participate, broadened their daily worship by choosing mainly theistic rather than Christocentric readings and hymns. Already, at Mahatma Gandhi's ashram, it was the regular practice to include in the daily prayer services hymns and readings from many traditions. When Gandhi founded the Phoenix Settlement in

South Africa, there were some Muslims, Christians and Parsis as well as Hindus amongst his co-workers. They used to sing hymns together from different traditions. The practice was continued at Tolstoy Farm and at the ashrams that Gandhi established after his return to India in 1914. Indeed Gandhi said of the Sevagram ashram that 'ever since the ashram was founded, not a single day has passed to my knowledge without this worship' (3). When Gandhi came to London in 1931, he conducted daily prayers in which people of several religions took part. Towards the end of his life he used interfaith prayer meetings as an important way of quelling communal bitterness and violence. Indeed he was assassinated on his way to such a prayer meeting.

In Britain, Unitarians were probably the first to include in their services readings from other scriptures besides the Bible. As early as 1924, Will Hayes published privately for his Chatham Unitarian Church *A Book of Twelve Services*. The services were universalist in conception and expressed Hayes' belief that the religion of the future would be a world religion. A later service, 'Every Nation Kneeling', was used quite widely, especially at occasions of the World Congress of Faiths. From the first days of the World Congress of Faiths, Will Hayes worked closely with its founder, Sir Francis Younghusband (4).

The World Congress of Faiths

At the 1936 World Congress of Faiths, the final session included readings from the scriptures of the world. A booklet was published of hymns which were sung on occasion during the Congress. The choice of hymns is interesting. Whilst taken from the Christian tradition, they were chosen in the hope that many members of other faiths also would feel able to sing them. They were 'Pour out Thy Spirit from on high', 'Gather us in', 'God is working his purpose out', 'Lord while for all mankind we pray'. 'Turn back, o man', 'To Mercy, Pity, Peace and Love'. 'Gird on Thy Sword' and 'The God of Love'.

In Britain, it was the memorial service for Sir Francis Younghusband, the founder of the World Congress of Faiths, which was one of the first public services in which members of different religions read from their scriptures. It was almost certainly the first such service to be held in an Anglican Church - taking place at St. Martin-in-the-Fields on the 10th of August 1942.

By the early fifties, an 'All Faiths' service had become a regular feature of the World Congress of Faiths' Annual Conference. Then, in 1953, in response to Queen Elizabeth II's request at the time of her coronation that people of all religions should pray for her, a public service was arranged.   Thereafter, for many years, the World Congress of Faiths arranged an Annual All Faiths Service.   Distinguished figures were asked to give the address, including the Indian High Commissioner Mrs Vijaya Lakshmi Pandit, Sir Basil Henriques, Sir John Glubb, the Hon. Lily Montagu and Dr Edward Carpenter.

In 1958, the service was held for the first time in an Anglican Church, at St. Botolph's, by invitation of George Appleton who at the time was vicar there.   The preacher was Dr Aurabinda Basu, a Hindu who was a lecturer at Durham University.   In 1961, the service was held at St. John's Wood Liberal Jewish Synagogue.   Ten years later it was held for the first time in a Roman Catholic Church, at the Church of the Holy Rosary in Marylebone.   The preacher was Fr. Tom Corbishley who insisted that the service was an act of worship. Despite the differences between religions, there was enough in common, he said, to come together in worship.   In 1972, for the first time, the preacher was a Muslim, Al Haj Sheik M Tufail.

The most memorable services perhaps were when the Dalai Lama spoke, once at the West London Synagogue in 1973 and again at Bloomsbury Central Baptist Church in 1981.   The latter service was held on a hot summer evening and the church was packed.   At the start everyone was asked to offer his or her neighbour a greeting of peace.   This created a relaxed and happy atmosphere.   In his sermon, the Dalai Lama said he disliked formality.   Neither birth nor death were formal !   He said we needed variety of religions, just as we like variety of foods.   Each has a particular insight to share.

Other Organizations

Increasingly by the seventies interfaith services began to be arranged in Britain not only by the World Congress of Faiths and by some Unitarian Churches but by other organizations, such as the Guide Movement, the Scout Association, the United Nations Association, the Red Cross, the Young Men's Christian Association and the Young Women's Christian Association.   All these organizations promoted moral and spiritual values.   Having come together to develop their physical, intellectual and moral growth, there came a time when participants wished to share their spiritual growth through corporate prayer or worship.   Whilst some organizations claimed a religious basis for their work, their membership was not restricted to adherents of a particular religious denomination.   If they were to arrange religious activities or services, these, because of their membership, had to be inclusive and acceptable to all and, therefore, multifaith.

Developments within the Guide Movement may be taken as an example. Every three years the World Association of Girl Guides and Girl Scouts holds a Conference in different host countries attended by delegates from well over a hundred nations. The religious basis of the Association was defined in 1972 when it was agreed that belief in 'a power outside oneself, a force greater than man' was the fundamental and unifying factor among its seven million members world-wide.

After a week of 'conferencing', during which old friendships are renewed, new ones made, hopes and fears shared and the aims of the Association to help girls and women to grow in mind, body and spirit are discussed in the differing contexts of the social, political and religious situations of the member countries, the delegates invariably feel the need to participate in some form of acknowledgment of their own beliefs and spirituality. In this context Guiders and Scouters from different faiths join together in moving and sincere acts of worship through which they express their commitment to the aims of the Association.

Similarly at national, regional or county level within the United Kingdom, when Guiders get together for conferences, seminars and training events, they often feel the need to re-commit themselves to the aims of the Guide Movement in an act of worship, a period of guided meditation or through suitable prayers. And where, as is now often the case, there are Guiders from more than one faith community present, care is taken that all present can participate fully in such an act of commitment. Such a principle is also encouraged in the local units of Rainbows, Brownies, Guides, Rangers and Young Leaders when girls from different faith communities are members, so that each girl feels that her own religious belief is of equal validity, and is recognized and respected by all other members of her unit. The multifaith character of the membership determined that the worship also would be multifaith.

'A Matter of Controversy'.

By the mid-sixties the question of 'interfaith worship' was just beginning to become a matter of controversy. Although the debate was mainly between Christians, it is helpful for people of any faith who wish to arrange a service to be aware of Christian sensitivities and the possible difficulties of holding a multi-faith service in a church.

In 1965 a 'Ceremony of Religious Affirmation' was arranged at St Mary-le-Bow to mark the opening of the Commonwealth Arts Festival. The event, which was attended by Prince Philip, included readings offered by representatives of each of the great world religions. The following year the first Commonwealth Day Multifaith celebration was held at St Martin-in-the-Fields. It was attended by the Queen.

The next year, however, following objections by some Christians led by Rev Christopher Wansey, Vicar of Roydon in Essex, the celebration was moved to the 'neutral' Guildhall, where it was held for a few years. Then in 1972, it moved to Westminster Abbey. The Abbey, despite some opposition, has continued to be the venue for this annual occasion, which is still usually attended by the Queen.

1967 also saw considerable controversy about the WCF Annual Conference service which was held at Great St Mary's Church, Cambridge. The vicar of the church, who had agreed to preach, was Canon Hugh Montefiore. He had attracted some adverse publicity earlier in the summer by remarks about Jesus' sexuality. Rev Christopher Wansey again led the protests and sent a telegram to the Archbishop, who was abroad. The Bishop of Ely allowed the service to proceed and in the event only a handful of protesters gathered outside the church.

Opposition within the Church of England to 'multi-religious services' had already been voiced in the Lower House of the Canterbury Convocation in 1966, when, after a poorly attended debate, Rev E Stride's motion expressing concern was approved. In the following year, 1967, the General Secretaries of the larger Anglican Missionary Societies strongly advised local churches not to provide for inter-faith services. The matter was taken up by the British Council of Churches, which in 1968 agreed that churches should 'scrupulously avoid those forms of interfaith worship which compromise the distinctive faiths of the participants and should ensure that Christian witness is neither distorted nor muted'. (5). The final draft had read 'all forms of interfaith worship', but this was changed to 'those forms of interfaith worship' - a compromise I had suggested on behalf of the World Congress of Faiths.

The final report to the British Council of Churches made clear that Christians would not wish to compromise the uniqueness of Christ and that members of other faiths would not wish to compromise their convictions. 'The presupposition of any interfaith service must be the acknowledgement of our religious diversity rather than a presumption of some (lowest) common denominator ..... What needs to be stressed is the religious approach to life and the common endeavour to bring spiritual values to bear on all its aspects'. The Report suggested exchange visits to different places of worship and 'occasions on which those of different faiths do in turn what is characteristic of their own religion, enabling the others present to share to the extent to which they conscientiously can'. The latter suggestion seems to be the genesis of what have become known as 'serial interfaith occasions', when members of different faiths in turn offer prayers on a chosen theme (6).

The World Congress of Faiths publicly welcomed the British Council of Churches' recognition of the changed situation in Britain. It also pointed out that WCF itself was careful in its services to ensure the 'distinctive witness of all participants'. The statement added that many of those attending interfaith services experienced a new awareness of God and found that their own particular faith had been enriched by contact with other faiths.

In view of the public debate, the World Congress of Faiths asked a working group, under the chairmanship of Dr Edward Carpenter, then Archdeacon of Westminster, to prepare a justification for the services which it arranged. As the opposition to such services was being voiced by some Christians, the WCF report, drawn up by Christians who were sympathetic to interfaith activity, was primarily addressed to Christians. The Group, however, asked the opinions of members of other faiths. These opinions differed, but there was a preference for members of one faith visiting another place of worship rather than for all trying to arrange a joint service. The report emphasized the Mystery of the Divine, who transcended the descriptions and names familiar to any one faith tradition. The moral values shared between religions were also emphasised. The Report summarized the objections of opponents and tried to answer them (7).

In 1977, *Inter-Faith Worship?,* a sensitive contribution by Peter Akenhurst and R W F Wootton was published. It gave a clear summary of the issues. The booklet cautiously accepted some forms of 'inter-faith worship', despite dislike of the term (8).

The growing discussion in the Church of England led to a demand for guidelines on the subject. An attempt to meet this request was made by a working group of the Archbishops' Consultants on Interfaith Relations, of which the secretary was Canon Peter Schneider. The Group's findings were published in *Ends and Odds* in 1980. A distinction was made, which has been widely accepted, between different types of services. The report distinguished, firstly, occasions on which members of another faith are invited as guests to the service of a particular faith community; secondly, interfaith gatherings of a serial multi-faith character; and, thirdly, interfaith gatherings with a united order of service. The report also included a useful section on visiting other places of worship.

The final paragraph summed up the view of the working group:

'Some Christians fear that participation in Interfaith services may lessen concern for the proclamation of the Gospel, may appear to equate religions or may obscure the uniqueness of Jesus Christ.   Interfaith Services, however, are occasional additions to the regular liturgical life of the Christian Church and not a substitute for it.   Interfaith is not a new religion.   The meeting which we welcome is of committed members of the Household of Faith.   Equality is of believers and not of beliefs.   We trust that as friendship and co-operation grows with members of Other Faith Communities, opportunities to share deepest convictions will increase.   Our common humanity, our ethical concerns and our recognition of the transcendent creates a bond.   The understanding of the Divine in the religions of the world is very different.   We believe, however, that God who has revealed himself in Jesus Christ is the God and Father of all people and that He is always greater than our understanding of Him.   We hope that in their proper place, Interfaith Services can help to give the Church a new vision of the greatness and glory of God and can strengthen Christians in welcoming, loving and serving others in the spirit and for the sake of Him who died for all mankind' (9).

The Committee for Relations with People of Other Faith of the British Council of Churches prepared a detailed response to the report of the Archbishops' Consultants.   Subsequently, in 1983, the committee published its own *Can we pray together ?   Guidelines on Worship in a Multi-Faith Society.*   This included a number of short contributions on relevant topics by different authors.   It is a suggestive and wide-ranging booklet, sympathetic to carefully thought-out interfaith prayer.   There is a particularly useful section on the value of silence, which, it is said, allows for a meeting in the presence of God   'at a level where words are inappropriate or simply inadequate' (10).

In 1991, a second Grove Booklet on the subject, *Interfaith Worship and Christian Truth* by David Bookless, was published.   At the time David Bookless was Assistant Curate at St John's Southall.   He began by describing various possible situations which might come under the umbrella term 'interfaith worship'.   He suggested that Christians had to balance the Great Commission to make disciples of every nation and the Great Commandment to love God and to love our neighbours as ourselves.   Those who stressed the first would object to interfaith worship, whereas those who stressed the second would have no problems with such worship. In conclusion, after mentioning the difficulty of the term 'interfaith worship', David Bookless suggested that it may give us a glimpse of heaven, where people of 'every nation, tribe, people and language' will worship the Lamb of God (11).

In the late eighties the discussion was taken up by the Inter-Faith Consultative Group of the Church of England's Board of Mission. A report *Multi-Faith Worship ?* was published in 1992. The booklet included a section on 'Some Theological Perspectives', which used the familiar classification of 'exclusivism', 'inclusivism' and 'pluralism'. Whilst warning of the dangers of syncretism and idolatry, the chapter acknowledges that 'a limited but positive place for some forms of "multi-faith worship" can be justified from the theological viewpoints which might most suggest caution' (12). The report distinguishes between visiting places of worship of Other Faiths, inviting guests of other Faiths to Christian services, serial multi-faith services and multi-faith services with an agreed common order. There is also a section on the legal position.

The Inter-Faith Consultative Group has also produced in 1992 a report on *The Marriage of Adherents of Other Faiths in Anglican Churches* together with guidelines on the subject (13).

General Synod in receiving the report *Multi-Faith Worship ?* asked the House of Bishops to give guidance to clergy and laity faced with situations described in the Report. This response was published in January 1993. In general, it restates the main points of the report, with perhaps more awareness of the legal constraints on any interfaith activity in Anglican churches or cathedrals. The final sentence says that 'practical wisdom suggests that the use of non-religious buildings avoids many of the difficulties which the use of churches may pose' (14). This reflects the threat of legal action by some evangelical Christians against Cathedrals which allowed interfaith services.

Some who made such threats were amongst the supporters of the so-called 'Open Letter' (15). This was a move by some Anglican clergy to close Church of England buildings to interfaith prayer, on the grounds that Jesus Christ was 'the only Saviour and hope of mankind'. The Open Letter particularly focused on the use of Westminster Abbey for the interfaith Commonwealth Day Observance. The 'Open Letter' was criticized in many quarters, particularly for the language and tone that it adopted. The Archbishop of Canterbury dissociated himself from it and, before its publication, wrote to its sponsors asking them to abandon a project which 'played on Christian fears about encounter with other faiths'. *The Times*, in a leader, reminded its readers that 'In the early church, Justin Martyr attributed all truths to be found in non-Christian religions to the Word of God who enlightens all. The faithful of all theistic religions could join in the prayer of St. Augustine of Hippo: "Our hearts are restless and will not rest until they rest in Thee" ' (16).

The Times leader also referred to the Second Vatican Council's 1965 *Declaration on Non-Christians*, which described all peoples of the world as having their own perception of 'a hidden power that hovers over the course of things and over the events of human life'. 'The Catholic Church', the declaration said, 'rejects nothing which is true and holy in these religions'. In Britain, Catholic concern for positive relations with people of other faiths has been shown in many ways, especially by the varied activities of Westminster Interfaith. This has arranged a number of interfaith occasions, including an annual pilgrimage, in which people of different religions have read from their scriptures or said prayers. Some of these events have been held at Westminster Cathedral, including a memorable celebration of the tenth anniversary of the Day of Prayer for Peace at Assisi in 1986. Brother Daniel Le Faivre, of Westminster Interfaith, has published valuable resource material for those arranging interfaith gatherings (17).

Several of the Free Churches in Britain have also appointed special committees to foster understanding of people of different religions. Some of these committees have given attention to the question of interfaith prayer (18).

Developments Outside Britain

Occasions when members of different religions come together for prayer are by no means confined to Great Britain. At the Vancouver Assembly of the World Council of Churches in 1983, members of various faiths were invited to participate in a Public Witness for peace and Justice. World Thanksgiving, which has a beautiful Chapel of Thanksgiving in Dallas, USA, has arranged a number of interreligious ceremonies on the theme of thanksgiving and issues an annual Declaration of Thanksgiving, which is endorsed by a leading member of each religion. International interfaith conferences of the World Conference on Religion and Peace, the Temple of Understanding, the International Association for Religious Freedom, the Assembly of the World's Religions and similar organisations usually provide times of devotion led by members of a particular faith to which all the conference participants are invited as well as some joint opening and closing ceremony (19). In India there has been a long history of times when people of different religions meet for prayer (20).

An event which attracted much interest was The Day of Prayer for World Peace at Assisi on October 27th, 1986. Religious leaders from around the world responded to the Pope's invitation to join him in a day of prayer and fasting for peace. The event was televised across much of Europe and widely reported in newspapers across the world.

The day began at The Church of St Mary of the Angels with a welcome from the Pope. He denied any intention of seeking a religious consensus or of making a concession to religious relativism. During the day, time was allowed for each faith community to offer its own prayers in different parts of the city. Then, in the afternoon, all made their way to the Lower St Francis Square. The ceremony began with the choir singing 'Da Pacem'. Then each faith offered its prayers for peace. The book of prayers stressed that 'each act of prayer, which is followed by a pause for reflection, is quite separate' (21). It was made very clear in the official literature that people were invited to be together to pray and not to pray together. The event was of 'a serial interfaith character'.

Cardinal Roger Etchegaray, President of the Pontifical Commission for Justice and Peace, insisted that no syncretism was intended. 'We have come from many religious traditions around the world, we come together in complete faithfulness to our own religious traditions, each well aware of the identity of our own faith commitment. We are here together without any trace of syncretism. This is what makes the richness and the value of this prayer encounter ..... What we will do now, offering our own prayers, one after the other, gathered in this place, should make manifest to all and to ourselves how, in the identity of each, we are all called to pray and work for the great good of peace. Differences are thereby not suppressed, but rather affirmed' (22).

Subsequent World Days of Prayer for Peace were held at Mt Hiei in Japan and at Mornington Bay in Australia and the tradition has been continued by the Fellowship of St Eggidio. The Assisi Day of Prayer for World Peace, together with the World Wide Fund for Nature's interfaith celebrations which were also held at Assisi (23) encouraged Roman Catholics and some Christians of other traditions to join more readily in interfaith prayer. In 1991, Pope John Paul II, recalling the Day at Assisi, called on Christians to join with people of other faiths in working and praying for peace (24).

Sharing Worship: Communicatio in Sacris

The most comprehensive discussion of the subject of multi-faith prayer is *Sharing Worship: Communicatio in Sacris*, edited by Paul Puthanangady. This was the fruit of a Research Seminar held at Bangalore, India from 20-25 January 1988 in which about forty scholars, mostly Indian Roman Catholics, participated. The book deals with Christian participation in the rituals of other faiths, the participation of both members of other faiths and of non-Catholic Christians in Christian rituals and the possibility of shared or interfaith prayer.

The keynote address was given by Fr D D Amalorpavadass, who was the founder of the National Biblical, Catechetical and Liturgical Centre [NBCLC] at Bangalore. He distinguished two approaches, the secular and the spiritual. The term secular in India does not imply irreligious nor antireligious attitudes. The Indian constitution is secular in the positive sense that all religions are treated equally and guaranteed freedom. Religious differences, however, have been exploited by some politicians so as to become a threat to national unity. Common worship may therefore serve as an antidote to communalism and reinforce the traditional Indian attitude of tolerance. Further it can serve to affirm human dignity and also offer a vision of a new society for which all can work together.

The second approach makes spirituality or religious experience the meeting point. This is because the 'deepest level of every religion is religious experience' (25). This, Fr Amalorpavadass suggests, is the authentic meeting point between India and Christianity, 'because the core of Christianity is mystical union and the core of India is God-experience' (26). Sharing in each other's worship is possible because of three characteristics of spiritual experience. First, God transcends any name or form; second, spiritual experience is ineffable and cannot be communicated; third, spiritual experience is a journey to the 'further shore' and inter-religious dialogue is also a pilgrimage. There can, Fr Amalorpavadass says, be 'a common worship corresponding to each stage reached together by the interlocutors of dialogue'. The form of such common worship thus depends on the depth at which members of different faiths are meeting. Although religions differ in creeds, doctrinal formulations and rites, they 'converge at the core level of religious experience and mysticism ..... so common worship can be a means for and an expression of authentic God-experience' (27).

The emphasis on mystical or spiritual experience which transcends the particularity of one religion is voiced by several other writers. Fr Gregory D'Souza from Mysore, concluded his paper with these words: 'Although religions are diverse with much difference as regards creeds, rites and scriptures, still as they move towards their core through religious experience and reach the kernel in mystical experience they all tend to converge. This proves that at a really authentic religious level of mystical experience there seems to be a common denominator. And this common denominator would lead us to an interreligious sharing in worship "communicatio in sacris" ' (28). Sister Vandana, a member of a Christian ashram, emphasized the silence beyond all religious practice. She began with the verse :

> As there is silence beyond sound
> > to which the sound is meant to lead us,
> As there is a stillness beyond movement
> > which the dance is meant to hold
> So there is a worship beyond temples, beyond mountains -
> > a worship 'in spirit and in truth' (29).

Together with an emphasis on meeting at the level of spiritual experience there is also, in this volume, a recognition that all religions are from God. The final report states that 'From the beginning till today God has been reaching out to humankind through his Spirit. He is at work in all religions and traditions' (30). It follows that the scriptures are also of God and it is fitting to read them in the Christian liturgy (31). Indeed, at a Seminar on Non-Biblical Scriptures, held in 1974, it had already been argued that 'the use of non-biblical scriptures would ultimately result in a radical reorientation of the Indian Church, and so help her to become a unifying force in the pluralism of India's religions and cultures' (32). The catholic hierarchy in India, however, had discouraged the practice. Notwithstanding, the Christa Prema Seva Ashram in Pune had continued to experiment in this area. Sister Sara Grant, in her important paper, described the experience of her community in the fourteen years from 1974 to 1988. This had confirmed the dynamic power of the Spirit at work when there is a sharing of scripture (33).

There is a careful discussion of the nature of sacraments and symbols. It is suggested that new symbols are needed to express a unity in the spirit. Whilst eucharistic sharing is primarily for those who are united with each other in faith and baptism, the final report suggests that it could be extended to those who are committed to Christ, but who fear alienation from their community if they were baptized. Eucharistic sharing might also be extended to those who 'moved by the Spirit are living by the Gospel values', especially those working closely with Christians and taking grave risks in the struggle for human rights and solidarity with the poor (34).

Attendance at Hindu rites is discussed and practical issues, such as whether the Christian should accept *prasad* or food which 'has been offered to an idol'. This leads into discussion of the meaning of idols. The possibility of a Christian accepting a Hindu as a 'guru' is discussed. The celebration of interfaith marriages is given some attention. It is recognized that most Orthodox Muslims would not encourage non-Muslims to participate in their official worship.

The volume also contains interesting contributions from Hindu and Muslim scholars and a clear account of Gandhi's prayer meetings. Mr S N Rao distinguished different forms of worship in Hinduism. The highest is the realisation that the Supreme Spirit and the individual Spirit are one. Constant meditation upon the divine within the heart is a lower form of worship. Lower still is singing hymns of praise to an external deity. Because of this acceptance of various ways of worship, Hinduism, Mr Rao claimed, is the most 'catholic ' of religions. To support this he quoted from the Bhagavad Gita:

> 'Whatever may be the form in which each devotee seeks to worship Me with faith, I make their faith steadfast in that form above (7, 21)'.

Hindus, therefore, he said, should have no problem in praying with members of different faiths (35). Although some temples restricted the entry of non-Hindus, this was only a matter of 'narrow orthodoxy, prejudice or ignorance' (36). The non-Hindu, however, should have a proper understanding of the role of idols, if their participation in Hindu worship is to open up genuine religious feelings in their hearts (37).

Fr Xavier Irudayaraj, as a result of a questionnaire, found that almost all Hindus asked supported interfaith prayer, especially as a way to strengthen social harmony and integration. They insisted that one's own faith is not contaminated or diluted by sharing in the worship of another faith community (38).

Professor S M Abdul Hameed indicated the problems for orthodox Muslims, who are required to give wholehearted allegiance to Allah, of joining in interfaith prayers. He mentioned, however, the Sufi tradition, which stresses divine immanence. He ended his comments with these words:

> 'Love, love of the Maker is the essence of Sufism and love is something that is human and it is love that makes man partake of the element of divinity. It may not be an exaggeration to say that to be divine one must first be human, because humanity leads

to divinity and divinity graces humanity. And so it is possible not withstanding whatever is felt and whatever is seen, the divinities in the temple or a church or a mosque or a synagogue or a Sikh Gurdwara, wherever we turn our face we find the same Being, being presented in different forms, with different labels. And common sharing is absolutely necessary not only for the survival of a particular philosophy or a particular religion including Christianity, Hinduism or Islam, but it is absolutely necessary for the survival of humanity' (39).

Whilst *Sharing Worship* addresses the Indian situation, it is recognized that this is an area where the Church in India has a vital and distinctive contribution to make to the life of the Universal Church.

Can Jews and Christians Pray Together ?

Christian-Jewish dialogue has also occasioned some joint events and some reflection on interfaith prayer. In 1990, for example, to mark the 800th anniversary of the Massacre at Clifford's Tower in York, an 'Expression of Heritage and Hope' was held in the Minster (40). At the Annual Conference of the Council of Christians and Jews members of each faith are encouraged to be present at a service of the other tradition.

Many Orthodox Jews are not willing to take part in interfaith services. Dr Jakobovits, then Chief Rabbi of Great Britain, explained why he was unwilling to attend the Day of Prayer at Assisi. Partly this was because the day chosen was the 'morrow of our final Holy Day in this season's festive period' but also 'because of our purely religious reservations on interfaith services, committed as we are to conducting our most intimate communion with our Maker in a form and language familiar to us by hallowed tradition stretching over thousands of years' (41).

At a meeting of the Inter Faith Network for the United Kingdom, Rabbi Julian Jacobs, who is adviser to the present Chief Rabbi on interfaith matters, echoed this view that 'prayer and worship are very personal matters involving the most intimate relationship between a human being and God. Orthodox Jews did not feel that it was right to share in joint prayer or worship with people from other communities'. He went on to say that members of other faiths were welcome to attend synagogue services, but would not be asked to take part. They might be asked to speak subsequently at a meeting in the hall. Equally Orthodox Jews would attend other places of worship but would not participate in the service. 'For example, the Chief Rabbi would attend the Commonwealth Day Observance held in Westminster Abbey, but was not ready to participate in it by taking responsibility for a reading. The passage from the Jewish scriptures had instead been read by a Reform Rabbi who took a different view of the matter. The former Chief Rabbi had also been present at the memorial service held in a Christian church for those killed in the Lockerbie air disaster' (42).

Progressive Jews are happy to take part in interfaith services. Rabbi Dr Albert Friedlander, in a letter to *The Times*, in response to the 'Open Letter' said 'An approach to God which is unable to see other religions reaching towards the infinite is a very fearful and weak faith. I believe totally in an interfaith approach, though one of course, that runs parallel to and does not conflict with the prayers in my own community. One does not surrender integrity and authenticity by meeting on separate occasions with one's neighbour and sharing prayers and goals which reach out towards the One God. God responds to the genuine quest within all human beings who prove by their actions that they believe in the vision of the Divine Kingdom which is open to all in the course of time' (43).

Besides the growing number of occasions when Jews and Christians meet for study and discussion together in Europe and North America (44), there are also personal occasions that bring Jews and Christians together. Although 'marrying out' is becoming increasingly common in the USA and in parts of Europe, it is discouraged by Jewish authorities. Some rabbis in the USA will take part in a religious ceremony, but the practice is not encouraged (45). In the USA, also, Christians and Jews sometimes come together to remember the Holocaust and have produced appropriate liturgies (46).

The Views of Members of the Different Faiths

The Inter Faith Network meeting, which has already been mentioned, was especially valuable because it provided participants with the opportunity to hear the views of members of several religions. In much of the previous discussion in Britain it is only Christian opinions that have been presented.

Councillor Amarjit Singh, a Sikh, spoke of his time as Mayor of Newham. As Mayor, he had tried to represent all the people of the borough, whatever their faith and had been happy to participate in the worship and celebrations of different communities. When he took up office, he arranged a civic service in his own local gurdwara. During this, there were readings from all the great religions. Dr Mrs Subadra Siriwardena, a Buddhist, pointed out that as Theravada

Buddhism is a non-theistic religion, Theravadin Buddhists could not take part in prayers or worship directed to God. Whilst she respected other religions, she could not take part in shared worship. Mr Mathoor Krishnamurti of Bharatya Vidya Bhavan said that as a Hindu he had no problem in joining in the prayers of any religious community because the Hindu religion was a universal religion. Maulana Shahid Raza of the Imams and Mosques Council (UK) said that some Muslims were discouraged from joining in interfaith activities by the possibility of being asked to take part in interfaith worship (47).

A Worldwide Concern

The practice of interreligious prayer is spreading and the world church is now beginning to discuss the subject. In 1993, the World Council of Churches' Office on Interreligious Relations set up with the Pontifical Council for Interreligious Dialogue, a study project on interreligious prayer and worship (48).

Both offices conducted a survey to ascertain how widespread is the practice of interreligious prayer and to discover the theological questions being discussed as a result of this practice. Although the response was uneven, the WCC had fifty replies, from eleven countries - Austria, Brazil, Canada, Germany, India, the Netherlands, South Africa, Sweden, Taiwan, the UK and the USA. The survey showed the great variety of occasions on which people joined with members of other faiths to pray. In Taiwan, Christians and Buddhists 'sang and prayed' at human rights meetings. In the USA, Jews, Christians and Muslims stood together in worship against the death penalty. In Brazil, members of different faiths have prayed together for those who suffer from Aids. Different forms of service were described. In Germany, a distinction was made between 'interreligious prayer', where the event is planned as a unity and 'multi-religious' prayer, where representatives of different religions say their own prayers, while the others are listening (49).

The Pontifical Commission's enquiries only received a limited response. Of 189 dioceses in the USA, 12 replied. The patterns of interreligious prayer these answers showed were very varied, although some form of interreligious prayer was common on Thanksgiving Day and on national holidays. Replies from India suggested interreligious prayer was quite common, especially in response to a crisis, on feast days and at schools. Answers from Canada suggested considerable caution.

In 1996 the Pontifical Council for Interreligious Dialogue and the Office on Inter-Religious Relations of the World Council of Churches jointly arranged a consultation in Bangalore. In their concluding statement, participants said that 'Christians should welcome opportunities to pray' with people of other faiths. 'Participation in interreligious prayer' they continued 'is not an optional activity restricted to an elite group, but an urgent call for a growing number of Christians today and should be a matter of concern for all Christians' (50).

Indeed, interreligious prayer should be the starting point of interreligious encounter in the view of Father Pierre de Bethune osb, who has been deeply influenced by Zen Buddhism and who is secretary of the Inter-Monastic Council. He told the consultation of the Trappists of Our Lady of Atlas, at Tibhirine in Algeria, who with Muslim friends created a prayer group called *Ribat es Salam* 'The Bond of Peace'. The first time a neighbouring Sufi community, at Christmas 1979, asked to meet the monks, its spokesman made clear that they wanted to meet for shared prayer. 'We do not want', he said, 'to engage in a theological dialogue with you, for it has often raised barriers which are man made. Now we feel called by God to unity. So we have to let God invent something new between us. This can be done only through prayer'.

Commenting on the experience of this group, The Prior of Tibhirine, Fr. Christian de Cherge, wrote recently, 'It is always somewhat painful to see a man of prayer and interior life stop short in his dialogue with the other, stumbling on enunciations of faith and the opacity of their incompatibilities, without seeking the other above in the heights or in the depth of the Spirit'. Tragically this dialogue through prayer was destroyed by the ruthless murder of seven of the Trappist monks, but the initiative has not been buried with them.

Evidence from the participants in the consultation suggested that interreligious prayer is increasingly common. The consultation was told of a group of Christians and Muslims in Zamboanga City in the Philippines who meet regularly and of a group of poor Christian and Muslim women in Delhi who gather regularly for prayer. Prayer does not require intellectual sophistication and, in situations of conflict, can override the divisions and bitterness, because as Fr Pierre de Bethune said, 'beyond all violence, prayer is the strongest bond, because it goes through God. It is the shortest way between humans, because God is the One who is nearest to us'.

Discussions suggested that whilst in some places, regular interreligious prayer takes place, more often it is arranged because of a special situation, for example during the Earth Summit in

Rio in 1992 or to mark the new political order in South Africa or the many gatherings to pray for peace during the Gulf War.

It was recognised that interreligious prayer - the term the group used for the whole phenomenon - takes many forms. Sometimes it may be quite informal: praying at the bedside of a friend of another faith who is ill or at an interfaith marriage. Visits of members of one religion to the place of worship of another religion happen quite often. The guests may be invited, in some way, to participate, which requires sensitivity and respect both on the part of the hosts and the guests.

The statement distinguished between 'united interreligious prayer' and 'multireligious prayer'. Multireligious prayer is when each religion in turn offers prayers. The advantage of this form of service was seen to be that the integrity of each religion and its distinctiveness is honoured. The disadvantage is that those present may most of the time be mere bystanders and not enter into the spirituality of the other.

Interreligious prayer, where there is an united order of service with some prayers or affirmations said together and perhaps some hymns which everyone is invited to sing, was seen to allow everyone present to pray together. The disadvantage is that the content may be reduced to a lowest common denominator (although it could be raised to the highest common factor) and may mask the uniqueness of each faith tradition. Such services, it was said, could be enriched by the introduction of new creative symbolic actions.

It was noted that some Christians have found meditation a point of meeting, whereas some Buddhists insist that their non-theistic meditation is quite different from Christian theistic meditation - indeed some Buddhists resent Christians borrowing their techniques.

This led to considerable discussion of the whole question of borrowing from another tradition. Quite a lot of Christians read devotionally the scriptures and prayers of other faiths. It was asked whether the Upanishads should be read in India at a Christian eucharist. If so, should the reader add 'This is the word of the Lord'. At some Christian ashrams, the eucharist includes the Hindu ceremony of *arti*, or passing the light, and the offering of flowers with the bread and wine. Yet, it was pointed out that the way in which Christians have appropriated the Hebrew Bible as pointing to Christ is resented by most Jews and some Hindus resent Christian adaptation of Hindu ceremonies.

Because words divide, it was recognised that silence is often a feature of interreligious prayer, although it may be used as a way to evade disagreement or dialogue. At the inauguration of President Mandela, prayers were led by the Chief Rabbi of South Africa, by a Hindu, a Muslim and by Archbishop Desmond Tutu. The daily proceedings of the South African Parliament now begin with a few moments of silent prayer, which Archbishop Tutu has strongly criticised as 'a cop out'.

Whilst the consultation focused on interreligious prayer, it was made clear that this could not be divorced from interreligious dialogue and practical co-operative action. In fact, interreligious prayer loses much of its meaning if there is no strong relationship between the participants.

It was recognised, therefore, that questions about interreligious prayer cannot be separated from theological discussion of the relation of Christianity to other religions. No one at the Bangalore meeting doubted that the Spirit is at work in other religions. There was, however, little discussion of theological questions nor of how to deal with Biblical texts that condemn idolatry, although one or two papers made comments on these subjects. The statement stressed that interreligious prayer is a significant part of the healing and reconciling mission of Christ. The statement also said that 'holding fast to the centrality of Christ, we urge careful theological reflection on our understanding of the uniqueness and universality of Christ'.

The statement made clear that neither multireligious prayer nor interreligious prayer was intended to create a new religion of 'interfaith' nor should either replace the regular pattern of prayer of a particular faith community. Interreligious prayer should be a symbol of hope and a reminder of God's purpose and promise for justice and peace for all people and a call to all people to offer themselves to be used in this work.

This was most vividly illustrated by a participant from Brazil who described a vigil that was held on Leme Beach to support 'Citizen Action Against Hunger and Misery, in Favour of Life' which is championing the cause of more than thirty million Brazilians who live in abject poverty. As the vigil ended, people were sent away with these words:

> Let's go now in peace,
> Let's live as free people.
> Let's build a free world,
> Let's build humanity, free, nurtured and creative,

who may be hungry not for food,

but for music, for poetry, for dance, for expression,

for love, for joy, for happiness, for a life of plenty.

Response to a New Situation

It is clear that the number of occasions on which people of different faiths meet in prayer is increasing in many parts of the world. In most cases the wish for 'interfaith prayer' arises out of situations in daily life. It is a creative response to new relationships for which traditional practices do not provide.

Certain distinctions about types of interfaith events are now widely accepted, although the best way of naming and describing the differences is far from agreed.

1. Services of a particular faith community to which members of other faiths are invited as guests.

> Here guests are present as observers and not expected to participate unless they choose to do so, perhaps by joining in the singing of a hymn. The normal service may be modified to make the guests feel more welcome. For example, explanations may be added. Perhaps one of the guests will be asked to give a message or to read. There are several occasions when a rabbi or an imam or other religious leader has been asked to preach at a Christian service. At a Sikh Gurdwara or a Hindu temple, for example, a visiting Christian minister might be asked to speak.

2. Interfaith gatherings of a serial multi-faith character. These are the occasions described at the Bangalore consultation, following a distinction made by the German churches, as multi-religious prayer, whilst an American Presbyterian report calls them 'focused observances' (51). They are what others describe as 'being together to pray'

> In these events a member of each faith present is invited to read or say a prayer. Usually the order of contributors is determined in terms of the alphabetical or chronological position of the faith. Although the readings may be on an agreed common theme, each contribution is distinct and there is no necessary assumption that members of other faiths present agree with this. Representatives of each faith make an offering to others of a reading or prayer or song that they wish to share. There

may be a simple symbolic act, such as the lighting of candles or offering of flowers to each other.

3. Interfaith gatherings with a united order of service. These are what the Bangalore consultation called interreligious prayer and what the American Presbyterian report called 'alternating worship and observation'. Others describe them as 'praying together'.

> These services are planned as a unity. The order of readings may be to bring out the theme. All participants may be asked to join in a prayer, or an affirmation or perhaps a hymn. There is likely also to be a symbolic act to express the sense of unity.

Mention has also been made of personal occasions, such as a wedding involving partners who belong to different religions. Because such occasions raise particular questions, they are not discussed in detail here although some of the general considerations are relevant. These considerations are also relevant to School Assemblies if they are of a multifaith character, although there are also legal issues and educational questions arising about collective worship as part of the school day.

The form that multi-faith prayer takes depends upon the participants and their particular situation. It will also reflect their intention for the event and perhaps also their view about the relationship of religions to each other.

3.   THE ISSUES

Marcus Braybrooke

The pioneers of interfaith services had a desire to encourage a sense of the unity of religions. In recent years, many of those who have taken initiatives have clearly acknowledged the distinctiveness of the historic faiths.

'Universalist in conception'.

Will Hayes saw his services as 'to some extent a confession of faith. They are universalist in conception'. In his Preface to *Every Nation Kneeling,* he referred to a passage from one of Whitman's private notebooks, which summed up the idea behind the services. 'There are (those) that specialize a book, or some one divine life, as the only revelation. I, too, doubtless own it, whatever it is to be a revelation, a part, but I see all else, all nature, and each and all that to it appertains, the processes of time, all men, the universe, all likes and dislikes and developments - a hundred, a thousand other Saviours and Mediators and Bibles - they too (are) just as much revelations as any. The grand and vital theory of religion ..... must admit all, and not a part merely' (1).

Sir Francis Younghusband, whilst recognizing the differences between religions, stressed the underlying unity. 'We need never lose our faith', he wrote, 'that all the time there may be an underlying and overarching harmony which may reconcile them all, if only we could reach it' (2). Here is the mystic's sense that the reality of the Divine transcends the particular and limited understandings of any one historical faith. It was a view voiced by Bishop George Appleton at a WCF service when he said, 'We stand in worship before the mystery of the final reality to whom or to which we give differing names, so great and deep and eternal that we can never fully understand or grasp the mystery of His Being' (3). This position is held by many Unitarians and Universalists and by modern Hindus such as Ram Mohun Roy and other members of the Brahmo Samaj, by Gandhians and by Vedantists. Swami Tripurananda of the Ramakrishna Vedanta Society, for example, recently quoted at a WCF conference, words of Swami Vivekananda. Vivekananda said he had learned from his master Sri Ramakrishna that 'the religions of the world are not contradictory or antagonistic. They are but various phases of one eternal religion. There never existed many religions, there is only one' (4).

Baha'is also stress the essential unity of religions. As a Baha'i contributor to this volume says, 'Because the central teachings of the Baha'i faith are the Oneness of God, the Oneness of Religion and Oneness of Mankind, Baha'is find it easy to fit in with the format of interfaith worship and do not see it as in any way compromising their beliefs'. Baha'u'llah urged his followers 'O people! Consort with followers of all religions in a spirit of friendliness and fellowship .... inasmuch as consorting with people hath promoted and will continue to promote unity and concord, which in turn are conducive to the maintenance of order in the world and to the regeneration of nations' (5).

The emphasis of the Indian publication, *Sharing Worship*, on spiritual experience as the meeting point, also suggests that believers may discover a unity beyond their differences.

To those who have this sense of the essential unity of religions there is no real problem with interfaith services. The differences reflect the variety of human thought and culture. Those who pioneered interfaith services were mostly of a universalist outlook and this may be partly why these services were regarded with suspicion by the more orthodox. They felt that a certain view of the relation of religions which they did not share was being presupposed and, sometimes, imposed.

'Committed Members of the Household of Faith'

The growth of interfaith services in recent years has been because a growing number of committed members of a faith find themselves in a deepening relationship with committed members of other faiths. The meetings are, as the Archbishops' Consultants put it, 'of committed members of the Household of Faith' (6).

The starting point is not a presumed underlying unity. Rather it is how people who are conscious of their differences may adapt the worship of their religious community to make space for members of another. Is there enough agreement between members of different religions to give any meaning to joining together in prayer? Is the attempt to pray together a search for a common denominator so low that it is largely vacuous or an expression of the highest common factor?

People may also be concerned for their religious integrity. By participating in prayer with members of other religious communities, does a person hide or betray his or her own beliefs or appear to endorse other people's beliefs, which she or he does not share?

'One God'

Those who defend interfaith services may say that all are worshipping the same God. This, however, raises two questions. The first is whether there is sufficient common understanding of what is meant by 'God' to make the occasion significant. Secondly, does this allow for the participation of non-theists, such as Buddhists?

'We all meet in the one God', said Canon Hugh Montefiore, who later became Bishop of Birmingham, when as Rector of Great St Mary's Church, Cambridge, he welcomed people to a WCF All Faiths service there. He suggested there are four stages in our meeting with people of other faiths. First, there is learning about what they believe. Then, there is reflection about what this new knowledge means to us. Then comes the confrontation, when we are stripped naked and grapple with each other in our agreements and disagreements. Then, 'beyond doctrines and convictions, we move into the reality of God Himself'. We retain our religious identity. 'We simply acknowledge that we are all creatures of the one God, his Spirit is in us all, we all experience the one God, that all our lives are lived in him. As our different prayers and scriptures in this service witness, we experience before him human sinfulness and awe: we offer to him human thanksgiving and gratitude: we place before him human desires and hopes: we receive from him all that is good and beautiful and true. To deny the propriety of common worship seems to me almost a blasphemy against the One God who made us all, and it is certainly a denial of our common humanity' (7).

If it is accepted that there is One God and that people of many faiths seek to worship that God - although this view is challenged by some Christians such as Tony Higton (8) - it can also be said that people do not have to agree to everyone else's picture of that God. Part of any interfaith service is a listening to the beliefs of others. Only when some words are said together need there be the supposition of agreement. David Brown, who was Bishop of Guildford, in his address at the WCF service at St Martin-in-the-Fields in 1976 spoke particularly about the limitations of language. The most universal language, he said, is that which crosses the frontier between the Eternal and the contingent. This may be why sometimes it is most helpful to meet in prayerful silence.

The second concern is the rejection by most Buddhists and Jains of belief in a Creator God and in intercessory prayer. Addresses to a Creator God or requests for divine favour and help will be unacceptable. At the Chicago Parliament of the World's Religions in 1993, some Buddhists made a protest on this point. At the 'Assembly of Spiritual and Religious Leaders', Ven Samu

Sunim of the Zen Buddhist Temple in Chicago read out a statement in which he complained about the theistic assumptions of many who spoke at the Parliament. 'With great astonishment we watched leaders of different traditions define all religions as religions of God and unwittingly rank Buddha with God. We would like to make it known to all that Shakyamuni (Gautama) Buddha, the founder of Buddhism, was not God or a god. He was a human being who attained full Enlightenment through meditation and showed us the path of spiritual awakening and freedom. Therefore, Buddhism is not a religion of God. Buddhism is a religion of wisdom, enlightenment and compassion' (9).

Buddhists, however, do recognize a transcendent dimension to life and Buddhism is widely considered to be a religion. Acknowledgment of 'The Truth' may be acceptable. Ven Vajiragnana in his article in this book suggests that prayer may be thought of as meditation - a way of cleansing the mind from selfish desires and of developing spiritual qualities such as loving-kindness and compassion (10). At some interfaith services a prayer has been used based on the Buddhist 'radiating' prayer or meditation.

Perhaps, if Buddhists and Jains are willing to share in multi-faith services which avoid imposing theistic presuppositions, others who reject a theistic standpoint may also be willing to participate, especially if the emphasis is on human unity and shared moral values.

'The Uniqueness of Christ'.

A particular concern for some Christians is that interfaith services appear to deny the uniqueness of Christ and blunt the missionary command 'to make disciples of all nations, baptising them in the name of the Father and the Son and the Holy Spirit' (Mt 28 19). Linked to this may be concern for the feelings of converts to Christianity, who may wonder if the sacrifices that they had to make were worthwhile.

There is no single 'Christian' position on the relationship of Christianity to other world religions (11). The subject is a matter of vigorous debate. Many Christians, however, now recognize that, whilst for them God's definitive self-revelation is in Jesus Christ and that he is of universal significance, other religions have their own validity and are channels of divine revelation. Such Christians are happy on occasion to join in prayer with members of other faiths (12).

Human Unity

For some the greatest value of interfaith services is their witness to human unity, despite religious differences. This is likely to be the emphasis of services held during One World Week. Multi-faith services may be a shared witness against racism and all that threatens human rights. They may also be an expression of a common commitment to help the hungry. Some services, especially those on United Nations Day or during the Week of Prayer for World Peace, will focus on the yearning for peace to be found in each faith tradition. Others will emphasize shared concern for the environment and the valuing of the natural world in all the great faiths.

The affirmations at The Commonwealth Day Observance are of this character. At different stages in the proceedings, members of the congregation are invited to stand and to say together:

> We affirm our respect for the whole of the natural world and acknowledge our responsibility for exercising our stewardship with care and consideration for all its elements.

> We affirm our common faith in the dignity and unique worth of the human person independent of colour, class or creed.

> We affirm our common faith in the need to establish justice for every individual, and through common effort to secure peace and reconciliation between nations.

> We affirm our common faith in the need to assert the supremacy of love in all human relationships.

> We affirm our membership of the one human family and our concern to express it in service and sacrifice for the common good. (13).

Conclusion

The debate within several faith communities about interfaith prayer is likely to continue, because of the growing number of situations where people consider this possibility. It is hoped that this book will help to clarify the issues and make people more aware of the particular concerns of members of different religions.

Fr Amalorpavadass, in his keynote address to the conference on 'Sharing Worship', as we have seen (14), distinguished two motivations. One stressed the need to affirm human solidarity, the other put the emphasis on meeting at the deepest level of spiritual experience. The two approaches, however, as he said overlap. Many of those who have taken part in interfaith services, perhaps initially with hesitation, have found them to be inspiring and moving occasions. They witness that their own faith has been deepened whilst their appreciation of others' faiths has been broadened. The experience of oneness in the presence of the Transcendent has been a powerful incentive to work for peace and justice, to seek to help those in need and to struggle to protect the environment.

Interfaith services are not intended to create a new religion nor to be a substitute for the regular pattern of prayer of any faith community. Rather they are special occasions which both acknowledge the rich diversity of humankind's spiritual traditions and affirm the unity of the human family.

4. DEVOTION AND WORSHIP IN THE BAHA'I FAITH

Hilary Freeman

Private prayer

'O Son of Light !

Forget all save Me and commune with My spirit.   This is of the essence of My command, therefore turn unto it', said Baha'u'llah.

Baha'u'llah has ordained daily prayer for His followers.   There are three obligatory prayers from which Baha'is may choose: a short prayer, to be recited between noon and sunset; one of medium length, which should be recited three times a day - in the morning, at noon, and in the evening; or a long prayer to be recited once in twenty-four hours.   The Short Obligatory Prayer is :

'I bear witness, O my God, that Thou hast created me to know Thee and to worship Thee.   I testify, at this moment, to my powerlessness and to Thy might, to my poverty and to Thy wealth.
There is none other God but Thee, the Help in Peril, the Self-subsisting'.   [Baha'u'llah]

In addition to the obligatory prayers, Baha'is are enjoined to pray and read the Holy Writings twice a day, in the morning and evening; and meditation is given equal importance with prayer. There is no set form for such prayer and meditation and believers are free to choose according to their own wishes.

'Abdu'l-Baha (the son of Baha'u'llah) writes:

Through the faculty of meditation man attains to eternal life; through it he receives the breath of the Holy Spirit - the bestowal of the Spirit is given in reflection and meditation.   Meditation is the key for opening the doors of mysteries ..... This faculty of meditation frees man from the animal nature, discerns the reality of things, puts man in touch with God.

This faculty brings forth from the invisible plane, the sciences and arts.   Through the meditative faculty inventions are made possible, colossal undertakings are carried out.
[*Paris Talks pp.174-176*]

'Abdu'l-Baha describes the state of prayer as bestowing life, and as being the best of all conditions.   However, prayer is not offered solely by means of reciting the sacred verses, either in privacy or during shared worship.   In the Baha'i Faith, work in the service of humanity is also elevated to the station of prayer.   'Abdu'l-Baha writes:

.....arts, sciences and all crafts are counted as worship .....   Briefly, all effort and exertion put forth by man from the fullness of his heart is worship, if it is prompted by the highest motives .....   This is worship: to serve mankind and to minister to the needs of the people.   Service is prayer.   A physician ministering to the sick, gently, tenderly, free from prejudice and believing in the solidarity of the human race, is giving praise.

[Baha'ullah and the New Era]

Congregational Prayer

As there is no clergy in the Baha'i Faith, there is no congregational prayer of the type found in some other world faiths, where the prayers are led by the priest and the congregation join in the responses.

There is only one instance in which Baha'u'llah commanded 'congregational' prayer and that is the Prayer for the Dead, in which one believer recites the prayer whilst all others present are required to stand.   Apart from the Prayer for the Dead, congregational prayer is forbidden by Baha'u'llah.

This does not mean to say that Baha'is do not gather together for shared worship, but that they would not recite prayer in unison.   Rather, each one reads in turn from the prayers and writings revealed by Baha'u'llah, His forerunner The Bab, and His son, 'Abdu'l-Baha.   An exception to this is found where prayers are set to music: choral arrangements of Baha'i prayers are permitted.

Types of prayer in the Baha'i Faith

As a tenet of faith, Baha'is believe that all the major world religions have come from the same Source and are part of one, evolving, progressive Revelation.   In their private devotions, therefore, and from time to time during shared worship, Baha'is will also read from the revealed Scriptures of other Faiths.

An individual Baha'i may, in his private prayer, use his own words directly from the heart, but would not normally do so in shared worship.   To Baha'is, the revealed Word of God is seen as having the greater power and efficacy.

Baha'is pray together frequently at many types of event.   They hold meetings of a purely devotional nature.   They may gather together to pray for a specific purpose: for the well-being of a member of the community who is sick, for example.   There is very little ritual in the

Baha'i Faith, and so prayers at weddings and funerals are very much the personal choice of the families involved. Commemoration of Baha'i Holy Days always includes a suitable devotional programme.

One of the most important gatherings for prayer in the Baha'i calendar is the Nineteen Day Feast. As its name implies, the Baha'i year consists of nineteen months of nineteen days. The Feast is held on the first day of each month. It is the occasion for regular consultation between the elected local Spiritual Assembly and the other believers in the locality. The programme of the Nineteen Day Feast consists of three parts. The first is entirely spiritual in character, consisting of prayers and readings from the Baha'i Holy Writings; the second is consultation, and the third, the material 'feast' and social gathering. The main purpose of the Feast is to foster fellowship, love and co-operation between the believers.

At the present time, Baha'i gatherings in most localities are held in the homes of the believers. Where a large community exists, they will either rent or purchase a larger property to serve as a local Baha'i Centre. Baha'i Houses of Worship (Temples) have been established in each continent. According to the teaching of Baha'u'llah, each House of Worship is open to the followers of all Faiths and the Holy Scriptures of all the major world religions are read in the House of Worship.

Sharing in Interfaith events

Baha'u'llah exorted His followers :
> 'O people! Consort with the followers of all religions in a spirit of friendliness and fellowship ..... inasmuch as consorting with people hath promoted and will continue to promote unity and concord, which in turn are conducive to the maintenance of order in the world and to the regeneration of nations ..... '(*Tablets of Bah'ullah,* pp 22,36).

Baha'is, therefore, have since the earliest days of their Faith, been eager for involvement in inter-faith dialogue and worship. The first mention of Baha'u'llah and His teachings in the West was made at the World Parliament of Religions in Chicago on 23 September 1893, in a paper presented by Revd Henry H Jessop. Baha'is have been involved with the World Congress of Faiths since its inception in 1936.

Because the central teachings of the Baha'i Faith are the Oneness of God, the Oneness of Religion and the Oneness of Mankind, Baha'is find it easy to fit in with the format of interfaith worship, and do not see it as in any way compromising their beliefs.

5. BUDDHISM AND PRAYER

Ven Pandith M Vajiragnana

The Buddha was very friendly with all the other religious teachers of his day, and he even visited them from time to time.   He did not reject them or become unfriendly towards them. He showed that Buddhists can meet and co-operate with followers of other religions on matters of spiritual, moral, social and economic importance.   There are, however, two items of doctrine about which they cannot compromise.   The first is the idea of a creator God, and the second is the idea of an eternal soul, both of which have no place in the teachings of the Buddha.

Buddhists do not accept the idea of a creator God who controls everything and governs man's destiny.   According to theistic religions, however much you practise virtue and morality, you cannot liberate yourself without the grace of God.   Therefore, God's grace is fundamentally important in these religions.   This means that you are not your own master.   In Buddhism, however, you are your own master.   'Oneself is one's own master.   Who else can be the master ? ' (*Dharmapada*, v.160).

Let us examine what common ground we may discover in the matter of prayer.   For many people, prayer might be said to be a solemn and humble request either to God or to an object of worship.   It might be said to be a respectful attempt to strike a bargain with some deity or higher power, asking either for guidance or intervention on one's behalf.   One tenders so much faith, or so much self-denial in mild forms of asceticism, in the hope of receiving substantial benefits, either here or hereafter.   It is an understandable instinct for man to turn to prayer in times of need or perplexity, but for a Buddhist this definition of prayer is not acceptable.

As I have said, Buddhists do not have a belief in the existence of a supreme, omnipotent god who can influence the outcome of events.   To a Buddhist, the world is subject to the operation of five natural laws, which we call *Niyama*, but these laws operate by themselves and cannot be varied at the request of any beings, either human or divine.

One of these five laws is *Kamma*, the law of cause and effect.   Good actions produce good results, and harmful actions produce harmful results.   If we want to experience desirable effects, we must create the right causes.   This moral law is impersonal, and cannot be swayed by any request made by man.

If the Buddhist does not believe in the existence of an omnipotent deity, then there is no point in making petitionary or intercessory prayers.   The Buddha said that neither the repetition of holy scriptures, nor self-torture, nor the repetition of prayers, penances, hymns, charms, mantras, incantations and invocations can bring us real happiness.   Instead the Buddha emphasised the importance of making individual effort in order to achieve our spiritual goals. He likened it to a man wanting to cross a river; sitting down and praying will not suffice, but he must make the effort to build a raft or a bridge.

The Buddha once said to one of his prominent lay-disciples, called Anathapindika,

> 'There are, O householder, five desirable, pleasant and agreeable things which are rare in the world.   What are those five ?   They are long life, beauty, happiness, fame and (rebirth in) the heavens.   But of these five things, O householder, I do not teach that they are to be obtained by prayer or by vows.   If one could obtain them by prayer or vows, who would not do it ?
> 'For a noble disciple who wishes to have long life, it is not befitting that he should pray for long life or take delight in so doing.   He should rather follow a path of life that is conducive to longevity.' (*Anguttara Nikaya*, v.43)

He goes on to recommend the same course of action in respect of the other four desirable things.   The path which should be followed is that of generosity (*dana*). morality (*sila*), and mental culture (*bhavana*).   These are the foundations of the Buddhist way of life.   If we act rightly, then we shall experience wholesome effects in accordance with the law of *kamma*.

It is up to each individual to take the appropriate steps to achieve both spiritual (and also material) progress.   The Buddha said, 'You yourselves must make the effort.   Buddhas do but show the way.'   On another occasion he counselled his followers, 'Be ye islands unto yourselves.   Be a refuge unto yourselves.   Take to yourselves no external refuge.'   His last words were, 'Work out your salvation with diligence.'

I suggest that it is in this process of spiritual development that we can find another definition of the word 'prayer'.   The spiritual path is one of purification, the cleansing of the mind of all negative qualities, such as greed, hatred and ignorance, which cloud our vision and prevent us from seeing the Truth.   For the Buddhist, meditation is the primary tool for training the mind to give up its selfish, egotistical desires.   In the Dhammapada it is said, 'Empty this boat, O monk.   Emptied by you it will move swiftly.   Cutting off lust and hatred, to Nibbana you will thereby go.' (v.369)   Buddhism is primarily a mind culture and it is this process of mental purification which might be described by the word 'prayer'.

Most prayer is for gain, but in meditation the reverse is true.   It is undertaken in order to reduce our cravings and desires, it is a process of inner transformation and improvement.   The Buddha emphasised the importance of meditation as a means of promoting self-discipline, self-control, self-purification and self-enlightenment.

Meditation may also be used to develop the four spiritual qualities of loving-kindness, compassion, sympathetic joy and equanimity.

People sometimes ask what Buddhists are doing in their devotions if they are not 'praying' in some sense of the word.   The Buddha was not a god and we do not worship him.   He was not a creator, destroyer, or preserver of the universe;   neither was he a dispenser of favours, nor a supreme punitive power.   He was, however, a peerless teacher and we respect him accordingly.

Traditionally, offerings are made to the statue of Buddha which is to be found in every shrine room.   It is important to realise the true significance of these offerings, since to the non-Buddhist this may appear to be nothing better than mere idol-worship.

The offerings take the form of flowers, lights and incense.   When making these, the mental state of the devotee is very important.   The flowers are offered with the full awareness of their impermanence and that they will soon fade.   So too the sweet smell of incense will also fade.   This symbolises the transiency of all conditioned things.   The candles or lamps symbolise the dispelling of the darkness of ignorance by the light of wisdom.   Strictly speaking these external objects of homage are not absolutely necessary, but they are useful and help to concentrate one's attention.   They are offered as a mark of gratitude for what the Buddha taught us, helping us to reflect on his virtues.

Other devotional activities involve the recitation of the supreme qualities of the Buddha, of his teachings and his noble disciples.   The Buddha's discourses may also be recited.   All these activities are instruments of mental purification and they represent prayer in its purest form.

Buddhists will frequently participate in multi-faith events, acknowledging the diversity to be found throughout the world in its multifarious religious traditions.   The Buddha strongly criticised those who condemned the beliefs of others and stated that any such condemnation will only bring discredit, both to those who broadcast such criticism and to their own religion which they are attempting to glorify. Therefore, it is extremely rare to find a strong negative response to an invitation to attend an Interfaith occasion, or to an invitation to witness an act of worship of a different religion.

A problem does arise when a Buddhist is asked to speak on a platform where, for instance, all of the panel are described as 'Believing in God/the Transcendent/the Infinite'. Reword the theme and we shall be present !

Buddhists believe that every truth and every 'heavenly' state of being is within the grasp of humankind. We believe that there is nothing that cannot be understood through wisdom, and that there is no superior influence, power or being necessary to develop that wisdom and to guide us to perfection. It is only a matter of our own mental development. We each have full power and sole control over our own destiny.

People are social beings. Every individual needs association with others of his species. We need the companionship of like-minded people. Social intercourse is essential. We can all benefit from the company of others who have lofty spiritual aspirations and from those who regulate their personal lives in order to create harmony.

Worship, in the sense of 'adoration', is not a Buddhist activity. Yet in the more liberal sense of the word 'to show profound religious devotion and respect' there can be no objection. If, however, multi-faith worship consists of the former, then - although we may be present - we do not involve ourselves in the strong sentiments of witness.

With this in mind, I believe in the importance of the widest participation in most multi-faith occasions. It is not only through tolerance but also through altruistic love that peace and harmonious understanding can prevail.

6. CHRISTIANITY AND INTERFAITH WORSHIP

John Pridmore

Where Christians take part in interfaith worship, or allow it to take place in their churches, it is usually out of courtesy rather than conviction.   When half the Scouts are Sikhs it seems rude to forbid their prayers at the parade service.   However, while good manners may be a good reason for inviting those of other faiths to pray with us, there are better reasons for doing so, reasons which rest, not on liberal sentiment, but on the bedrock of Christian belief about Christian worship.

There are four distinct and essential characteristics of Christian worship which can be claimed to justify Christians in taking part in worship with those of other faiths, whether by attending their acts of worship, by welcoming them to Christian services, or by participation in interfaith observances.   For Christians worship is corporate, the criteria of its authenticity are ethical, it is our primary response to God and it is always situational.   The implications of the first and second of these features of Christian worship will be indicated only briefly.   The third and fourth considerations, that we worship long before we define our creeds and that our worship is always in a given context, will call for a fuller discussion.

A corporate activity

Christian worship is essentially a corporate activity.   I can pray by myself but normally I will worship with others.   When I worship I am already alongside someone.   That other person may be a baptised and communicant member of my church who affirms with conviction his or her faith in the words I use, meaning by them the same as I do.   Or he or she may have made no such commitment and remain deeply agnostic about some central claims of Christian faith.   Or again, my fellow-worshipper who says the same creed as I do may understand much of it quite differently.   I do not know what my neighbour believes, how well he or she believes, or whether the words of the creeds we share mean the same to him or her as to me.   Nor, most Christians would hold, is it my business to find out.   To that extent the Christian Church already accepts in practice that those who worship together need not share the same faith. Most Christian church services are to some degree acts of interfaith worship.   To be reassured that all are of one mind who take part in Christian worship would mean subjecting those present to tests of confessional conformity.   To be sure such scrutiny has been known in some Christian traditions but it is foreign to the spirit and custom of most.

Ethical

Christian worship is ethical or it is not worship at all. Christians believe that worship must issue in a life given to the service of God's kingdom. It is a central conviction of the scriptures which Christians share with Jews that worship unaccompanied by justice is unacceptable to God (Hosea 6.6, Amos 5.21-24, etc). What invalidates worship is not that those who pray together may profess different faiths but that they prove indifferent to the needs of their neighbours. 'Not everyone who says to me, "Lord, Lord," shall enter the kingdom of heaven but he who does the will of my father who is in heaven' (Matthew 7.21). The liturgy of worship matters but what matters more is the life of the worshipper. The ultimate criteria of true worship - and here Christianity draws deeply from its Jewish roots - are not liturgical but ethical. To refuse to pray with those whose lives testify to the authenticity and integrity of their worship is only possible by ignoring this prophetic tradition, fundamental to the understanding of worship in both Judaism and Christianity.

The Primary Response to God

Worship is our primary response to our experience of God, prior to its expression in creeds. Worship is the ground of faith. Our worship certainly reflects what we believe but, more fundamentally, it is our faith which is shaped and fed by our worship. We are constrained to worship before we compose our creeds. Christian worship is the heartbeat of Christianity. It supplies the oxygen for the Christian mind which goes on to formulate intellectual statements of Christian faith. 'Lex orandi, lex credendi'. The fashioning of our creeds and other propositional expressions of the Christian faith follows from 'the divine encounter' in prayer and worship. Thus there is an inherent contradiction in presuming to determine on doctrinal grounds who may or may not worship together. We discover from the experience of worship itself what are its proper boundaries.

Those boundaries may have to be redrawn as our experience of the presence and activity of God is enlarged. It was the firm conviction of the first Christians that Gentiles were inadmissible to the Christian church. The church was obliged to change its mind on this matter after a group of Christians found themselves present at a meeting where 'the Holy Spirit was poured out even on the Gentiles' (Acts 10.45). Here was manifestly authentic worship and the church had no choice but to think again about who were those with whom it might properly associate. 'Truly I perceive that God shows no partiality, but in every nation any one who fears him and does what is right is acceptable to him' (Acts 10.35).

The particular lesson of this experience was that Gentiles could become Christians without first having to submit to the requirements of the Jewish law, not that Christians may worship side by side with those of different faiths. What is relevant to the issue of interfaith worship is the fact that the church changes its mind about where to draw a line between the included and the excluded and it is made to do so in the light of its experience. The old wineskins of settled attitudes about the admissible and inadmissible are broken by the new wine of the work of God in unanticipated ways.

Much discussion about interfaith worship has become entangled in the meshes of the debate about revelation and salvation. Is God made known exclusively and finally in Jesus Christ and is authentic prayer and worship possible only for those who explicitly confess Christ as saviour ? Or is the truth of God, uniquely manifest in Christ, nevertheless revealed to the adherents of other faiths and the salvation of Christ available to them ? Or are all our religious stories equally vehicles of that transcendent reality whom we name God and do all the many paths of salvation ultimately converge on him ?

There is no prospect whatever of Christians coming to a consensus on this issue. But if we recognise the principle of 'lex orandi, lex credendi' and allow that it is the experience of worship which shapes doctrine rather than doctrinal pronouncements which govern worship, we may avoid the thickets of this dispute. It is in our meeting with God and with one another that we discover who are the ones with whom we may pray, not by consulting our creeds and catechisms however important these are as attempts to articulate our understanding of God.

Situational

Christian worship is situational, anchored in a given place and time. Worship is always inescapably contextual. It takes place somewhere and not somewhere else. It may be caught up into eternity - here on earth it starts at half-past-ten. No act of Christian worship takes place in a social vacuum, unaffected by the character and events of the world around. Even sectarian patterns of worship which seem to take no account of any social context, which express instead an individualistic other-worldly pietism, are reflections of society in their very rejection of it.

When we worship we lift up our hearts to God but our feet stay on the common ground of our one world when we do so. Within the mainstream of Christian tradition worship has always been seen as an offering of that world to God. The life of the world which we offer to God can no longer be limited to that of the shared experience of the local homogenous community. Of course we have always belonged to a wider world than our local neighbourhood but the extent of our interrelatedness and interdependence today is far greater than ever before. In many of our communities followers of other faiths literally live next door but today's media and modern methods of transport and communication have made the planet so small that those on another continent are scarcely any further away. Our neighbourhood is not the world. If worship is the offering of our world to God it makes no Christian sense to exclude from that worship the neighbours - whatever their religious persuasion - with whom we share that world.

Worship takes place within the context of the life of the world and is an offering of that shared life to God. One fact about that world, bearing directly on the issue of interfaith worship, is that it is a place of pain. That is not new. What is new, and what constitutes a seismic shift in the context in which worship is offered, is our awareness of the world's pain and the requirement that we take responsibility for it. Every war today is a world war. Every famine is a world famine. And neither the shrapnel nor the hunger discriminate between those of different religions. Where the world's pain is felt acutely enough to drive men and women to cry to God that prayer will not be contained in the factional and partisan channels of our different religious allegiances. Some of the most moving examples of interfaith worship have been those occasions where, locally or nationally, people of different faiths have come together in response to some emergency or disaster and turned together to God, by whatever name they know him. Few who have shared in such worship would doubt its validity. It would be a denial of the fundamental principle that faith is fed by worship to oppose such occasions on doctrinal grounds.

Christianity, for all its apparently exclusive claim, is open to the possibility of interfaith worship because of those essential conditions which must be met if worship is to be true. It is what belongs to the heart of worship as Christians know and practise it that allows Christians to join in prayer with those of other faiths. None of this is to suggest that such shared worship will always affirm all that Christians hold dear. Worship is a many-splendoured thing and the splendour of what Christians do together in, for example, celebrating the Christian eucharist is not the same as the splendour, let us say, of shared silence with those of different faiths. But if worship is indeed the very heartbeat of the Christian body to confine its expression to exclusively Christian forms and to exclusively Christian company is a potentially fatal hardening of its arteries.

7. HINDU WORSHIP AND PRAYER IN THE CONTEXT OF INTER-FAITH WORSHIP

Ranchor Prime

To understand Hindu worship it is important to be familiar with the underlying principle of Hindu prayer which can be summed up in the sequence *sravanam kirtanam vishnu smaranam.*

'Sravanam' means Hearing. Prayer begins with hearing of the sacred.   When I hear a sacred sound, such as a name of God or a description of the activities of God, or of holy persons devoted to God, my attention is drawn towards God and my soul is inspired.   'Kirtanam' means Chanting.   Speaking or singing about the divine is the essence of prayer.   By using my tongue to sing hymns or mantras glorifying God, or to describe the path to God, my heart is focused on the divine.   After hearing and chanting comes 'Smaranam', Remembering. Hearing and chanting about Vishnu leads to remembrance of Vishnu.   To remember God at all times is the essence of all spiritual instructions.   This principle is not just reserved for the temple or place of worship, it is for anywhere and anytime.   Constant spiritual remembrance leads to a life of service to God, where every action is sanctified by the thought of the divine and the worshipper carries God in his or her heart.   As Krishna says in Bhagavad Gita: 'Those who remember me without deviation obtain me easily because of their constant engagement in devotional service.' (8.14)

The hearing-chanting-remembering principle is reinforced by the addition of 'satsang', the company of holy persons.   Hearing is especially effective if it is from a holy person who has love for God.   Furthermore, hearing and chanting are both enhanced if they are shared in the company of other worshippers.   All worshippers can be considered as lovers of God.   Such group sharing or 'satsang' is the basic activity of worship in any Hindu temple.

Considering this stress on the act of hearing and chanting, most Hindus would feel a natural sense of community with all who gather to worship God, regardless of their particular faith. They would have an empathy and sensitivity to hearing the words of another's faith in God, or even, as in the case of Buddhism, another's words of insight or instruction on the spiritual path, because so much of Hindu worship is composed of just this - hearing inspirational words or sacred hymns from spiritual teachers or just from other worshippers.   Hinduism has a long tradition of giving honour and hospitality to any person of faith and such honour brings grace to the one who offers it to a sincere person of the spirit.

Another feature of Hindu worship is its multiplicity. In many ways Hinduism has always been its own multi-faith society. The Hindu tradition recognises that God appears in many forms at many different times and teaches many paths. Even the Bhagavad Gita, the central scripture for the majority of Hindus today, teaches at least three paths. Variety has always been a necessary part of Hindu tradition, which recognises that each of us is an individual with particular spiritual needs. Perhaps this is in part due to the belief in re-incarnation, because it assumes that the journey to God is longer and more demanding than can be encompassed by most of us in a single lifetime. Further, the cosmic context of Hinduism is far-flung. Hindu scriptures teach that there are many levels of reality and on all of them worship of God is going on. On higher planes there are 'devas' or demigods, who have been given greater powers than us and can themselves grant boons to their worshippers. On these higher planes are types of worship and faith that do not exist here, or at least only partially. And beyond these higher planes is the Svargaloka, the heavenly abodes of different gods such as Brahma and Indra, all of whom have their devotees. Within Hinduism there is also the basic division between worshippers of Shiva (Shaivites) and worshippers of Vishnu (Vaishnavas), as well as others who worship the Goddess Durga in one or other of her many manifestations. All this means that Hindus are naturally at home in the multifaith or interfaith world. Yet ultimately, the theistic Vaishnavas and Shaivites believe in an eternal Kingdom of God which lies beyond all other planes of existence. A simple devotion to the supreme God of Grace, whatever name he may be known by, is therefore esteemed as the highest expression of spirituality, as described in Bhagavad Gita : 'Giving up all other paths just surrender yourself to Me. I will release you from all your sins. Do not fear.' (18.64)

Finally, a word must be said about Hindu deity worship, sometimes wrongly called idol worship, which it decidedly is not. An idol is something set up in place of God (there are plenty of idols all round us today) whereas the image of the deity in a Hindu temple is made strictly according to ancient scriptural tradition to represent God in a form which the worshipper will recognise. The temple becomes the home of the deity, a place of sanctity where devotion and service to God are focused, where the great invisible Spirit becomes visible to allow the ordinary devotee to offer prayers and service and to see the otherwise unseeable form of God. It is a place where the visible and the invisible, the tangible and the intangible, meet. To think that the deity is simply a statue or idol is to make a travesty of this ancient tradition. For the most part Hindus welcome outside visitors to their temples, as one would welcome a visitor to one's own home. All they would ask is that the visitor respect the devotions and prayers which are offered to the deity for what they are: simple acts of devotion to God on the part of ordinary people of faith.

8. THE PRAYER IN ISLAM

Imam Dr Abduljalil Sajid

Prayer is the essence and manifestation of faith. It is the symbol of humble reverence before the Creator of the heavens, the earth and everything above and below. In the Holy Qur'an Allah (Subhanhu Wa Taala) says: 'Establish regular prayer, for prayer restrains from shameful and unjust deeds, and remembrance of Allah the Creator is the greatest thing of life without doubt'. Prayer is the pillar of Islamic faith, the mainstay of its conviction, 'the chief of good works and the best act of obedience', said the Prophet of Islam, Muhammed, peace and blessing of God be upon him. 'On the day of Resurrection, **three** people will find themselves on the ridge of black musk. They will have no reckoning to fear, nor any cause for alarm while human accounts are being settled. **First**, a man who recites the Qur'an to please God, Great and Glorious is He, and who leads the Prayer to the people's satisfaction. **Second**, a man who gives the call to prayer in a Mosque, inviting people to God, Great and Glorious is He, for the sake of His good pleasure. **Third**, a man who has a hard time making a living in this world, yet is not distracted from the work of the Hereafter.'

Said the Prophet, on him be peace and blessing of God:

'There are five Prayers which God has prescribed for His creation. For those who perform them properly, without disrespectful omissions, there is a guarantee that God will admit them to Paradise. To those who do not observe them, however, God offers no such guarantee: he may admit them to paradise, as He wills. 'These five times of prayer may be compared to a stream of fresh water, flowing in front of your house, into which you plunge five times each day. Do you think that would leave any dirt on your body?' When they replied: 'None at all!' The Prophet, on him peace, said: 'Indeed, the five Prayers remove sins, just as water removes dirt. When My servants ask you concerning Me, I am indeed close to them. I listen to the prayer of every supplicant when he calls Me. Let them also, with a will, listen to My Call, and believe in Me: that they may walk in the right way.'

The Prophet Muhammed said that prayer is one of the five pillars upon which Islam is raised. Just as a building loses its stability when one of its pillars falls, neglect of prayer will cause a person to lose his sense of morality and piety.

The institution of Prayer has been completely and perfectly established by the Holy Prophet Muhammed, peace and blessing of God be with him. In prayer a Muslim asks Him to guide him to the right way of life, and to help him overcome all forms of corruption, shameful behaviour and evil thoughts in order that we may be happy in this life and in the hereafter. Prophet Muhammed felt so strongly about the institution of prayer that in one of his last directives to his followers before his death, he emphasised the importance of safeguarding and promoting its observance. Prayer in Islam is a beautiful exercise in meditation through which a Muslim is able to forge a direct link with God. Thus it is not only an obligation, but also a gift and privilege. When a person neglects the worship of God he loses contact with Him and his sense of direction in life becomes faulty. He loses spiritual guidance that comes from submission and obedience to God and a person may become an easy prey for the evil influences of selfishness which confront every soul throughout every aspect of daily life. The spiritual vacuum created when prayer is neglected is soon filled with greed, prejudice, envy and other sins.

Where there is no prayer there can be no purification of the soul. It cleanses inner being, giving a fresh outlook on life and release from self-deception and conceit and an outer expression of an inner condition of belief and trust. The Holy Prophet once said : 'What stands between a man and disbelief is the abandonment of his Prayer to God'. Prayer in Islam is truly an act of worship to God. Worship means serving and obeying God in all aspects of life. Worship means that whatever is done in the world, it should be in accordance with God's guidance. Whether we sleep, wake, eat, drink or work - in fact, whatever activity we do - we are worshipping God if these activities are done in love of and obedience to Him. Performing the prayer regularly serves as a repeated reminder to the Muslim during the day and night of his relationship with his Creator. No matter how faithful an individual may be, such reminders are essential, for man's involvement in his human concerns and activities is so engrossing that it is very easy to lose sight of one's relationship with God, his place in the total scheme of things, his responsibilities, and his ultimate goal. It is precisely for this reason that worship does not require giving up the day to day world and sitting in a corner chanting God's name. For Islam is not a mere matter of doctrinal faith; it is a way of life to be lived in practice. Islam means surrendering to God and fighting against evil. Its essential message is : always remain prepared to obey God at a moment's notice. The Prayer, five times a day tests again and again whether a Muslim is prepared for this noble cause. Those who claim to be Muslims are tested to see whether they can put their claim into practice. If they cannot, their faith is of little value to Islam. For only they find the prayer hard and unwelcome whose hearts are devoid of reverence to God and who are not ready to live in submission to God.

Regular observance of Prayer is an excellent training for punctuality, and obedience to God in other commandments. Prayer involves a Muslim in community life, serious study, strict discipline, and true faith in the Creator. Mere verbal adherence to the creed of Islam is not enough. Prayer is an accepted practical expression for making a statement of faith. Basically prayer in Islam consists of recitation from the Holy Qur'an and glorification of God accompanied by various bodily postures. The five times of worship correspond to the five periods of the day: daybreak, noon, afternoon, the close of day, and night, corresponding to the organisation of man's time around various activities. In addition to this, through the bodily postures of the prayer, which consist of standing, bowing, prostrating and sitting, repeated a specified number of times in each prayer, the Muslim expresses submission, humility and adoration of God Most High with his entire being. The heart which is filled with the love of God, indeed has an urge to express all these feelings in physical as well as verbal form. By means of an established prayer, which enlists the participation of man's total nature, Islam provides the means of expression, in an extremely dignified and moving form, for these needs and feelings. Indeed, the self-discipline which is needed to perform prayer regularly and at the proper times - to perform the ablution before the actual prayer, and to carry on these prayers in the early morning when sleep is so attractive, during the busy daylight hours when one is busy with work, family and other activities, and at night when one is tired and wants to relax or sleep - reaffirms the human being's total dependence on his Creator and his position as His servant. Thus Prayer is truly the complete expression of man's voluntary submission to God. Man gets spiritual pleasure and enjoyment from prayer. With prayer, man thanks God for His Love, Mercy and Favours which, by developing his inner self, lend purpose and meaning to it. Purposeful prayer diverts man's attention towards God and gives him a wonderful feeling of the divine Presence. The Holy Prophet once said: 'There is no prayer without presence of mind and prayer is an ascension for believers.'

A Muslim is required to pray at the fixed times wherever he may be - whether in a Mosque, in his home, at work, or in any other clean environment indoors or outside - but it is preferable to pray in congregation with his fellow-Muslims. In such a congregational prayer, in which Muslims stand in straight rows shoulder to shoulder as one body united in the worship of God, the elements of discipline, brotherhood, equality and solidarity are very strongly expressed. It should be borne in mind that God does not need man's prayer, because God is Free of all needs. God is only interested in human beings' prosperity and well-being in every sense. When God commands and charges the Muslim to pray regularly, he means to help us; because whatever good we do is for our own benefit, and whatever offence we commit is against our own souls. It is possible to hide from the world but not from God. Muslims should come together to form strong communities to help each other in their life Mission : serving God, obeying Him, observing His Laws and promulgating it in the world. Prayer may be said to be supplication and praise. Proper worship of God is a degree of perfection not attainable by anyone.

The Qur'an taught Muslims to build good relations with all people of the world (Ch 49, v 13), spread peace everywhere and whenever it is possible (Ch 2, v 208 and Ch 8, v 61), cooperate in furthering virtues and God-consciousness (Ch 5, v 2) and to secure human welfare, good relations, justice and virtue (Ch 4, v 114).   The divine message has repeatedly enjoined them to be sociable and universal.   They should not be locked in a ghetto of land or mentality whether built by others or by themselves.   The Qur'an also teaches that such a strong commitment for a Universal reformation of human ethics on religious grounds which is basic for any other reform, has been the common responsibility of all the followers of the Divine revelation through successive Prophets: 'Among the followers of earlier revelation there are upright people, who recite God's message through the night, and prostrate themselves before Him.   They believe in God and the Last Day and enjoin the doing of what is right and forbid the doing of what is wrong, and vie with one another in doing good work, and they are among the righteous' (Qur'an 3: 113-115).   However, Muslims worship the One and only God. Association of any other being or object with the one God is a serious sin in Islam.   Therefore, Muslims may attend any collective worship where the one and only God is being praised.   The Qur'an condemns strongly any division among believers in the One God and the followers of His Divine messages (23:53).   May God lead all true believers in Him to fulfil one's heavy responsibility through mutual understanding and cooperation.   AMEN!

9. JAIN PRAYERS

Vinod Kapashi

Jainism is a path which leads one to achieve freedom from the shackles of attachment and aversion.   Jain scholars have always maintained that attachment to worldly things is the cause of karma or bondage.   This path explains and shows the way of true freedom and this is why it is a way of life, an ideology which transcends argument and logic - an ideology which makes sense.

The philosophy of Jainism has been studied through many many centuries.   It is a simple philosophy.   A person cannot attain happiness without distributing comforts and happiness to the people and animals around him.   One cannot achieve peace without sharing the ideals of universal love with one's surroundings.   In this way people will live in perfect harmony with nature.   One is advised to see Godhood in everybody because each one of us has a potential to achieve that supreme status. This is a status of enlightenment.

Jains believe in 24 enlightened souls or Tirthankaras.   The last to live on this earth was Mahavira who was born in 599 BC and died (attained nirvana) in 527 BC.   Mahavira was born on the thirteenth day of the bright half of the month Chaitra.   His real name was Vardhaman. He later came to be known as Mahavira (Great and brave), as he had conquered his inner passions and gained victory over all attachments. This is more than a victory in the battlefield. Though born as a prince, Mahavira left his royal household, gave up his worldly possessions and became a monk when he was 30 years old.   He spent twelve and a half years in meditation and practising non-violence and self control.   He obtained infinite knowledge when he was 42.   He spent thirty years in teaching the principles of ahimsa (non violence), self control and austerities.   He had also provided guidelines for lay people too.

Jainism is a dharma reflecting the true nature of our inner consciousness which manifests itself in practical life.   It is not dogmatic and does not believe in an almighty creator but believes in the potential to become an enlightened soul.   It is the path of right perception, right knowledge and right conduct leading towards 'the ultimate'.

Most Jains worship the images of Tirthankaras and pray to or praise the virtues of the Tirthankaras in various temples.   Of course one need not go to a temple to pray or worship. One can do this in a quiet room in a house or any other place a person may choose.

Prayer or worship is the expression of one's devotion.   A worshipper feels happy at the sight of his beloved image and momentarily he loses himself in complete devotion.   He forgets his worries, his problems, even his whole existence.   He starts praising and singing.   He admires and performs all sorts of adoration.   Sometimes a layman gets more peace and joy by some sort of ritual worship than by reading scriptures which he may not even understand.   In one way the whole idea of image worship does not fit into the Jain ideology of renunciation.   Jain Gods or Tirthankaras are Vitraga Gods (those who have no attachment or aversion).   They are also liberated souls not having any desire or any form and therefore do not grant any favours. This makes it seem strange that Jains have thousands of temples and they worship God with an intense devotion.

The whole thing can be explained from a different angle.   Worship is also a type of meditation (a Dharma dhyana)   Worship brings joy and peace, equanimity and love.   Idol worship in Jain religion is a very old practice, perhaps older than the Vedic tradition.   There is no reference to idol worship in the Vedas.   It is possible that idol worship in Hindu religion is an influence of traditions which prevailed in India before the arrival of Aryan people.

Daily Prayers include five acts of obeisance:

> *Namo Arihantanam* = I bow to the arihants - the ever-perfect spiritual victors;   *Namo Siddhanam* = I bow to the siddhas - the liberated souls;   *Namo Auariyanam* = I bow to the Acharyas - the leaders of the Jain order;   *Namo Uvajjayanm* = I bow to the upadhyayas - the learned preceptors;   *namo loe savva sahunam* = I bow to all the saints and sages everywhere in the world.

There is also a simple ritual of obeisance to God.   When a person enters a temple he or she pays respect with folded hands, bowing the head and saying *nishihi nishihi nishihi* (This signifies giving up all bad thoughts and egoistic attitudes).   A worshipper bows down in a systematic way and says :

> 'O compassionate one!   allow me to worship. With whatever capacity I have.   I bow with my head down.   Leaving behind ill feelings and sins.'

There are many worship-rituals too   *Chaitya-vandan* or worshipping the Lord in a temple, is a short and simple ritual.   It takes about five to ten minutes depending upon the song or songs rendered.   During evenings and after some rituals Aarati and Mangaldivo are performed.   This is a simple ceremony of waving a lamp or lamps in front of the representation of the Lord. People bid large amounts of money to have the privilege of doing such rituals.

Those who do not believe in temple-worship, perform other forms of worship by way of prayers and meditation.

Jains have a universal sympathy and this inspires them to seek fellowship with all people of faith.   This is expressed in a famous prayer :

'May all be happy
May all remain radiant in health
May all see beneficence
and may no one feel miserable.

I wish I had friendship and amity with all beings, a feeling of joy and appreciation at the sight of the virtuous; compassion for those who are in pain and complete equanimity in all situations adverse to me'.

10. A JEWISH VIEW OF PRAYER AND INTERFAITH SERVICES

Rabbi Rachel Montagu

The most important form of prayer in Judaism is the 'Amidah' or 'Standing prayer'. The destruction of the temple caused the enforced cessation in 70 C E of the offerings required as the service of God in the books of Leviticus and Deuteronomy. The rabbis therefore declared that the prayer services which had begun to be held in the prototype synagogues at the same time as the offerings in the temple, should replace the sacrifices, and this 'service of the heart' became the approved form of worship of God.

The prayer starts with three blessings of praise of God, and ends with three blessings of thanksgiving. In the middle on weekdays are thirteen blessings of petition, asking God for knowledge, the ability to repent, forgiveness, individual redemption, healing, prosperity, freedom for all, a just world, the passing away of evil from within us, the well-being of the righteous of the community, the peace of Jerusalem, Salvation, the coming of the Messianic Age and for a response to our prayers. This prayer is also called the 'Sh'moneh Esreh' or 'Eighteen'; originally it consisted of eighteen blessings; a nineteenth one praying for an end to sectarians was added early in the Middle Ages, and that has since been replaced by the prayer calling for an end to the evil within us.

On the Sabbath this prayer is said in a very abbreviated form; the prayers praising and thanking God remain, but the petitionary prayers are felt to be inappropriate on the Sabbath, God's day of rest, and are replaced by a single blessing thanking God for the gift of the Sabbath.

There was debate in rabbinic times as to whether there should be a fixed written form for this prayer; the rabbis usually felt that it should be a spontaneous outpouring of the heart and the ordinary people felt that they needed help and inspiration and a written liturgy would provide that. In the centuries since, the written form has become so fixed that a text is provided even for the moments of private meditation at the beginning and end of the prayer.

This prayer is said in the morning and afternoon services where it replaces the temple offerings and also in the evening. Because it is said facing Jerusalem, it has generated an art-form, the provision of embroidered or painted texts to hang on the wall most nearly facing Jerusalem.

There are two other elements which make up the basic structure of the synagogue liturgy. The Shema is the declaration of faith in God, and the commandment to love God found in Deuteronomy 6:4-9. It is said in the morning and evening service, together with Deuteronomy 11:13-21 and Numbers 15:37-41. It is preceded and followed by blessings which echo some of its themes; the commandment to love God and to teach these words to your children is balanced by a blessing reminding us that God loves us and has given us beautiful teachings. The commandment to say these words night and morning is balanced by blessings thanking God for creating the light and the dark. The theme of God's protection is reflected by a blessing asking God for redemption. Each synagogue service ends with the 'Aleynu' which hopes for the coming of the day when all will know God and worship him as One.

At formal services said in the synagogue with at least 10 people present, the morning and evening services begin with a call to prayer for the community. The services will be punctuated by and end with the kaddish, a prayer in Aramaic, the everyday spoken language when Hebrew had already become a formal language used for prayer and study. The kaddish is said especially by those in mourning although it does not mention death. These words of praise for God are thought to help the mourner return to life and hope.

The blessings at the beginning and end of the Sabbath, the whole Passover services and at least some of the rituals of the other festivals are home-based. It is said that the family dining-table replaced the altar in the temple as the place of worship.

The blessing is the basic Jewish liturgical form. Blessings are said at all times of day, over the performance of many of the commandments, before eating or drinking, after going to the lavatory, on seeing a rainbow etc. Each blessing begins 'Blessed are You, Eternal our God, Ruler of the Universe and continues with the form appropriate to the occasion. It says in the Talmud that it is praiseworthy to say a hundred blessings a day. The Grace after Meals, which consists of three blessings and some additional prayers, is regarded as very important because it is the fulfilment of a biblical commandment, 'And you shall eat and be full, and you shall bless the Eternal your God for the good land given to you.' (Deuteronomy 8:10)

The Psalms are used in Jewish liturgy, as part of the morning, afternoon, Sabbath and festival services, preceding the Grace After Meals and for private prayer and petition.

There are many other prayers and meditations and songs written over the centuries. These together with many suitable Bible texts, for instance the Psalms, may be more appropriate to bring to those multi-faith prayer services where everyone contributes from their tradition on a given theme than the fixed daily Jewish liturgy. Liberal, Reform and some Orthodox Jews are happy to take part in such services. All Jews except the ultra-Orthodox, including some who might find it difficult to take part in a multi-faith event, are happy to welcome non-Jews to synagogue services. Regular Christian services may not be so easy; for instance the custom in some churches of adding the words 'Glory be to the Father and to the Son and to the Holy Spirit' at the end of the Psalms is offensive to Jews. While the Lord's prayer is not intrinsically problematic, and indeed articles have been written connecting it to Jewish liturgy, most Jews will feel that these words have become such a statement of Christian identity that they would prefer not to say them. It is also worth bearing in mind that a service planned to be non-denominational, with specifically Christological references removed, may still have the flavour of a Christian service to Jews because of its cultural form - for instance standing up to sing hymns from the church hymn book - and their wish to be present but not to participate actively should not be taken as a rejection. It should also be borne in mind that while Friday and Saturday may seem ideal days for meetings or interfaith services, Jews who would be quite happy to participate on another date, will not feel this to be an appropriate activity on the Sabbath.

The Reform Forms of Prayer for Jewish Worship include a special **Prayer for Interfaith Meetings.**

> Lord of all creation, we stand in awe before You, impelled by visions of the harmony of man. We are children of many traditions - inheritors of shared wisdom and tragic misunderstandings, of proud hopes and humble successes. Now it is time for us to meet - in memory and truth, in courage and trust, in love and promise.

> In that which we share, let us see the common prayer of humanity; in that in which we differ, let us wonder at the freedom of man; in our unity and our differences, let us know the uniqueness that is God.

> May our courage match our convictions, and our integrity match our hope.

> May our faith in You bring us closer to each other.

> May our meeting with past and present bring blessing for the future. Amen.

11. INTERFAITH COOPERATION - A MATTER OF FAITH FOR SIKHS

Ranbir S Sandhu

The Principles of Sikhism as given by Guru Nanak, the founder, and his successors up to Guru Gobind Singh, emphasize equality of all people, respect for all faiths, and interfaith tolerance, understanding and cooperation as fundamental beliefs. All humankind is recognised as one. Plurality of faiths simply reflects divine revelation in different lands to different people in the language, idiom and metaphor best suited to them. Supreme faith consists of remembering God and being pure in conduct. God pervades all creation and all act in accordance with His will. A Sikh is always conscious of the nearness of God and believes in universal brotherhood. This realization can only come through love. Hatred has no place in Sikhism. A Sikh is self-reliant and believes in honest living and sharing the fruits of his labour with others. Service in humility is a basic principle. Men of God see God in everyone, their hearts are filled with love, and they do not see anyone as bad or evil. People call each other good or bad only in their ignorance. Sikhs not only respect the right of others to freedom of worship but, in line with the concept of the saint-soldier as the human ideal, they would be ready to die to protect that right for all.

The lifestyle of a Sikh is based on prayer and praise of God (*Naam Japna*) along with pure conduct consisting of selfless service in humility (*Kirt Karna*) and sharing the fruits of labour with others (*Waand Chakhna*).

Sikh Concept of God

(a) One God, Creator and Doer, pervades all.

The Sikhs believe in One God, Eternal, Creator Who pervades all; Without fear and enmity; Timeless; Never born; Self-existent, (realized) through the Guru's grace. This statement of belief, in full or in an abbreviated form, appears at the head of every collection of verses in Siri Guru Granth Sahib. While stating that no man can ever describe all the attributes of God, there are numerous verses praising God as the Creator, the Doer, and All-pervading.

(b) Unity of Creation and Creator

According to Sikh belief, creation is a manifestation of God Himself. He creates it, pervades it and all finally merges into Him. It does not have an independent permanent existence.

(c) Divinity of the Human Soul

The Sikhs believe that the human soul is part of God. If one understood this link with Divinity, one would be at peace: accept God's love and rejoice in His will.

(d) God controls Creation. All act according to His will

The entire universe does what it is given to do by Him and in the manner He wills it. It is a play within Himself that God has caused to occur and is watching.

Prayer

(a) Nearness of God and Guru

Prayer is not merely a recitation of prescribed words in a certain specified manner but a constant consciousness of the nearness of God and Guru and a constant reference of all our thoughts and actions to God and His wishes. This consciousness is necessary to acquire humility and development of love for all. It also provides the moral strength to avoid the traps of lust, anger, greed, attachment and ego. An example from Siri Guru Granth Sahib is:

> 'My friendship is with the One God and I love only Him. God alone is my friend and He is my only companion. I converse with God alone. He never has a frown on His face. He knows all that worries me and never turns His back on me. God alone, with the power to create as well as destroy, is my only adviser. He, who has His hand on the heads of all the givers in the world, is my only Giver. The One God, who has power over all, is my support. The Guru has placed his hand on my head and united me with God, the source of peace, the One who is Saviour of the whole world. O Nanak, one's heart's desires are fulfilled and one finds the True Name if the union is ordained (by God) to start with.'

(b) Meeting God through Love

The Sikhs believe that union with God and complete understanding of His love can only be achieved through love for Him and for His creation. Hatred for anyone has no place in a Sikh

heart.   The daily Sikh prayers includes the following verse describing the futility of all holy acts if they are devoid of love:

'What has a man gained if he closed both his eyes and sat in concentration like a crane (looking for fish) ?   What if he bathed at all the holy spots over the seven seas ?   He has lost this world and the other one too.   If instead he lived in sin, he wasted his life and got nothing for it.   Let everybody listen to me carefully, the truth is that only he who has loved (God and His Creation) has found God.'

Siri Guru Granth Sahib gives numerous illustrations of unconditional love within the experience of earthly creatures and seen in association of objects in nature.   One of the illustrations is the love of a child for its parent.   The child loves the parent and depends upon him/her for education, enlightenment and support.

(c) See God in Everyone.   Universal Brotherhood

God being the object of devotion and love, a Sikh constantly remembers that God pervades all and sees Him in everyone.   A person at peace with himself would see others in the same light and will not feel hatred or enmity towards anyone.

(d) Realization comes only through Divine mercy

Siri Guru Granth Sahib teaches us that the realization that God is near and pervades all can come only through God's mercy and Guru's advice.   For example:

'The Same One pervades all. Upon whomsoever He has mercy understands this.'

Different Faiths

All the creation is proof of God's greatness.   No faith that believes in prayer to God can be false.   They are all essentially the same.   Siri Guru Granth Sahib tells us:

'My King.   You are the Eternal Master, forever.   All that You create is true.   O King, who can we call false when there is no other ?   You pervade all beings.   All pray to You day and night.   They all ask you for things.   You are the one providing for all. Everything is under Your command, my King.   Nothing is outside it.   All the beings are Yours and You belong to all: they all merge into You.   You fulfil the hopes of all, all pray to You.   O Nanak's King, O my Beloved.   You are the Eternal One; keep me (in Your service) in whatever manner might please You.

Emphasizing the essential unity of faiths, Siri Guru Granth Sahib's words are:

'Don't say the Vedas and the Books (Torah, Bible, Qur'an) are false.   False is the one who does not study them.'

All faiths worship the same God using different names for Him and praising some special divine attributes.   All mankind is one.   The apparent differences in form are indicative of God's glory in revealing Himself to various people.   For example:

'The Vedas and the Books (Torah, Bible, Qur'an) all stand and worship You.   So many people are lying at Your door that they cannot be counted.   Numerous *Brahmas* and *Indras* with their thrones.   *Shivas* and incarnations of *Vishnu* sing God's glory and so do many *pirs* Prophets, *Sheiks*. and holy men.   You pervade all completely and are fulfilling Yourself in all.   Falsehood destroys and people can reach You only if they follow the correct way but we all do what You Yourself call us to do'.

Also in Dasam Granth Sahib, Guru Gobind Singh Sahib tells us:

'Some shave their heads and become *Sanyasis*, some become *Yogis*. some are celibate and some are known for continence.   Some are Hindus and others Muslims, Sunni or Shia.   Recognize all humankind as one.   The Creator and the Merciful, the Provider and the Gracious are the same God.   Do not, in error or doubt, accept any other.   All serve the One.   He is the One Divine Teacher of all, there is but One Form, let all understand Him to be the same Light.'

For a Sikh, there are no bad people.   All are created by God.   They may appear to be different but all are God's creation and part of God Himself.   Siri Guru Granth Sahib tells us:

'One God is the Master of all, there is no other.   When, through the Guru's grace, He resides in someone's mind, He manifests Himself in that person.   This entire creation is a manifestation of the Omniscient God and He is everywhere.   If one carefully studies the (Guru's) Word, how can one call anyone bad.   A person talks about good and bad people only so long as he is caught up in Duality (that the creation is separate from God).   One who has followed the way shown by the Guru has understood the Unity and is absorbed in God.'

Interfaith Understanding in Sikh History and Practices

Throughout history, Sikhs have been committed to religious harmony and interfaith cooperation.   Guru Nanak, the founder of the faith, was loved by Hindus as well as Muslims. He was referred to as the Pir of the Mussalmans and Guru of the Hindus.   While ordering the execution of the Fifth Nanak, Siri Guru Arjan Dev Ji, Jehangir the Mughal emperor in Delhi noted that not only Hindus but many Muslims had started to gather around him. The Ninth Guru, Siri Guru Tegh Bahadar Sahib, sacrificed his life for the right of the Hindus to wear the sacred thread and the saffron mark on their forehead even though he did not believe in those rituals himself. Siri Guru Gobind Singh Sahib writes about it as follows:

'He protected their (right to wear) the sacred thread and the saffron mark. He did this great act in *kalyug*. He did this for the sake of the sadhus: he gave his life and did not express pain. He did this for *Dharam*. He gave up his head but not his determination.'

The story of Bhai Ghanaiya Ji, a Sikh, providing water to the wounded enemy soldiers after a battle is well-known. When some Sikhs complained about this, upon questioning by Siri Guru Gobind Sahib, Ghanaiya Ji is said to have replied:

'Everywhere I see Your form, I see no other. You pervade all equally. I cannot tell friend from foe. In all places I see Your form. I do not see any difference among people.'

During the period of Sikh rule in Punjab, the people of all religions felt free to practice their faiths and to participate in administrative and political affairs of the state at all levels of responsibility. There was no pressure on any one to embrace the Sikh religion.

Sikh Gurdwaras have always been open to everybody regardless of religion, race, colour or caste. Gurdwaras have free kitchens that are open to all and everyone is treated as equal. Harmandar Sahib (The Golden Temple) has doors on all four sides signifying acceptance of visitors from all the four corners of the world. The Gurus spoke against hypocrisy and false emphasis on outer formalisms and practices of every religion but respected the right of all to profess their faith and serve mankind in their own ways. During many ups and downs in their history, the Sikhs have always respected the scriptures and places of worship of others. Many Hindus, to this day, routinely attend Sikh worship.

Recently, there has been a recognition among members of various traditions of the need for interfaith dialogue and cooperation. Everywhere this has happened, Sikhs, dedicated by faith to inter-religious respect, understanding and cooperation, have joined in enthusiastically, not only in celebration with joint worship, but also in raising their voices with others against violence and injustice.

Summing up

The Sikh view of interfaith understanding and cooperation emphasizes that God is the fountainhead of love and understanding: that He pervades all creation and all act according to His will: that all faiths are God's creation: and that conflict is caused by ignorance and hypocrisy. The Sikh religion lays down tolerance and love of humanity as fundamental principles. Rite and ceremony are only incidental and open to adaptation.

God created us all and fulfils Himself through our actions. Let us act so we are worthy of His love. Let us open our hearts; let us learn about each other; let us work to open the closed one-religion societies to free worship by others; let us work to resolve religious conflicts, wherever they might exist, in an amicable manner and not let greed make religion its instrument. God gave us the various faiths. Let us, of different faiths, join hands and together glorify Him and His creation. Let us, together learn to appreciate the mosaic of beliefs God has given us and rejoice in His Will. Let us, as Siri Guru Granth Sahib has taught us, walk together in close embrace as brothers.

12. ZOROASTRIAN WORSHIP FROM AN INTERFAITH PERSPECTIVE

Shahin Bekhradnia

The purpose of Zoroastrian worship is to celebrate life and give praise for the wondrous creations of the world, to contemplate good and to deprecate evil.   The vehicle for some of these activities is prayer while particular rituals or meaningful actions may replace or complement prayer.

As Zoroastrianism is a monotheistic religion, most of these activities are directed towards *Ahura Mazda*, the Wise Lord.   However, Zoroastrians also recognize a number of important *yazatas* or guardian angels who, as manifestations of God's creative spirit, have given their names to each day of the month and each month of the year.   There are prayers or *yashts* which are translated as hymns of praise in honour of a number of the more important *yazatas*. On the day (or day and month) which carry the name of a particular *yazata* an individual may choose to recite the prayer dedicated to the *Yazata*.

Individual Acts of Worship

Zoroastrian worship consists of two sorts: communal acts of worship and individual acts of worship.   The individual acts of worship are more typically the recitation of certain prayers taken from the corpus of holy scripture known as the *Avesta*.   Traditionally this takes place five times a day at set times following the progress of the sun, always facing it or an alternative source of light and could be whenever an individual so chooses (realistically it is first thing in the morning and last thing at night with the other three *gah* not necessarily observed).   One of the prayers that is always recited is a confirmation of faith and those who wear the 'badges' of the religion, namely the *sedreh* (a muslim vest) and a *koshti* (a sacred cord) will untie and retie knots of commitment.   Other occasions for individual prayer might be a visit to the temple on a special occasion, or a visit to the resting place of a deceased beloved.   The other form of individual worship may involve ritual such as the lighting of a fire in a fire urn, and feeding it with myrrh, incense and sandalwood, sometimes circulating it around the rooms of a home while invoking blessings.

Communal Acts of Worship

There is also another form of worship which involves a senior priest and an assistant performing a high service or *yasna* (which comes from the root of the word which means to worship) on behalf of the community which symbolically purifies and re-envigorates the priests. This is normally a long service performed in the early morning on a daily basis where there are priests to do so, but few people attend these.

Zoroastrians have many communal celebratory occasions integrated into the religious calendar, most of which involve worship followed by eating together. Therefore whether the occasion is for example one of the six annual *gahambar* (endowment memorial feasts) or a service for a rite of passage, a priest or a number of priests will perform rituals centred around a fire urn, with the congregation joining in to repeat the most frequently recited prayers, *Asham Vohu* and *Yathha Ahu Vairyo*. Afterwards there will be communal prayer known as the *Hamazor* during which the participants traditionally confirm their shared faith, and renew bonds of solidarity by holding hands and reciting the prayer together. Most 'religious' gatherings are followed by a communal meal or a distribution of food.

Prayers are composed in languages that span over 2,500 years and most are by now incomprehensible to those who say them (like Latin and Church Slavonic). It is the power of intention with which they are imbued as well as their mantric dimension which is important. In Zoroastrianism the idea of worship, contemplation and nature are closely interlinked issues, since it is through meditation upon the harmony and regularity of nature that people are drawn towards an awareness of God and give praise to Him. Part of the worship therefore involves meditation upon God's creations and for this reason most of the religious celebrations are thanksgiving occasions. The ritual preparations that accompany the religious celebration consequently symbolise God's various creations such as opened seed bearing fruit like a pomegranate and sprouting wheat or lentil shoots. Apart from the communal occasions which require the presence of a priest, there are also informal, communal, religious events to which guests may be invited but with no priest and which are sometimes called 'Little Tradition' occasions which may be held in a home or at a shrine. Here prayers will be said sometimes after the telling of a story and a special altar or **sopra** with the manifestations of God's bounteous creation will be displayed. All these occasions offer the opportunity to promote good over evil by celebrating and identifying with 'pure' or life enhancing matter rather than with negative or 'impure' energies.

Zoroastrian attitudes to Other Faiths

In the distant past when Zoroastrianism was widespread throughout the Persian empires, the Old Testament records that Cyrus and Darius showed respect towards the Jews and their religious ideas. Similarly it is accepted by scholars that many ideas in Judaism concerning the Day of Judgement, and the Saviour at the end of the Time were absorbed from Zoroastrianism. After having conquered Egypt and Babylon we hear that far from enforcing an alien religion upon the new subjects, their religion was left untouched and that the Persian monarchs were happy to worship at their altars alongside them.

The idea then, of sharing a belief in the divine, in recognising that divine being as omnipotent and benign, was one of the guiding principles which allowed distant Zoroastrians to worship together with those of different cultural traditions, and it appears that there was no animosity between Zoroastrians and peoples of other faith. Indeed the ethos of tolerance towards other religions was such that one of the Sassanian kings married a Christian girl. Many of the scriptures indicate a time in the past when it was possible for those of other faiths to be welcomed into the Zoroastrian fold. People, who have heard that Zoroastrians have strict taboos about admitting outsiders to their religion or places of worship, might be surprised to hear that such a restriction is a relatively new idea in Zoroastrianism, originating in the mistrust and suspicion of those who have constantly persecuted Zoroastrians in the land of its origin, Iran or Persia.

The attitude of some 'orthodox' Parsees, (the Persian refugees who fled from Muslim persecution to India in the ninth century CE) does not admit outsiders even by marriage or adoption into the religion nor to take part in Zoroastrian worship on the grounds that they are 'impure'. This is not an attitude held by Iranian Zoroastrians nor by a growing number of more enlightened Parsees. However, it may be encountered and can be explained by the historical distrust and bitter experiences of the Zoroastrian communities at a time when the impure forces of evil were identified with those who oppressed them.

In more recent years Zoroastrians have had contact with more tolerant societies in which they are shown respect and not threatened. Indeed from closer contact particularly with Judaism, Christianity and Hinduism they have found many of their values, beliefs and practices reflected in those of other faiths. It is therefore in the ancient spirit of tolerance, respect and thanksgiving that Zoroastrians are beginning to participate in interfaith activities, happy to receive from and give hospitality to those of other faiths with whom they can join in worship.

13.   UNIVERSAL WORSHIP

'External worship, material worship, is the lowest stage; struggle to rise high for mental prayer is the next stage; the highest stage is where the Lord has been realised.

Even as we kneel before the image we repeat : 'Him the sun cannot express, nor the moon, nor the stars; this lightning cannot express Him, nor what we speak of as fire.   Through Him do they all shine' (Upanishad)

Every kind of worship is a necessary stage - 'the child is father of the man'.   Would it be right for an old man to say that childhood is a sin, or youth a sin ?   Man does not travel from error to Truth, but from Truth to Truth - from lower to higher Truth.   The whole world of religions is only a travelling, a coming up, of different men and women, through various conditions and circumstances, to the same goal.   A universal religion, then, is the sum total of all and still has infinite space for development.'

[This passage from a talk on Worship given by Swami Vivekananda at the 1893 World's Parliament of Religions was quoted by Swami Tripulananda at a WCF Conference on Multi-Faith Worship.]

14.   LOCAL INITIATIVES

RESPONSE TO A QUESTIONNAIRE

Jean Potter

Inter-Faith Groups

Inter-faith groups which have grown up in some of the multi-faith communities in Britain have often developed because people from different faith backgrounds, for whom their own belief is often of paramount importance, wished to find out more about people of other faiths. Learning about other faiths can then lead on to sharing cultural activities such as dance, music and food, providing the activity does not require any participant to compromise his or her religious belief.   When it comes to sharing in prayer or worship, however, there is often a fear that this will lead to compromise.   This is why many groups have felt unsure whether to embark on any form of inter-faith worship.

It was largely queries to the World Congress of Faiths from such groups or individuals as to the desirability, feasibility and practicality of arranging interfaith prayer or worship that prompted the production of this book, as a resource which might be of help to such groups or individuals.

To gauge the need for such a book, a questionnaire was initially sent to all known inter-faith groups throughout the country asking for their reactions, experiences and suggestions on the subject.   Replies were received from 18 groups, and without exception all felt that such a book would be useful.

Some groups have given considerable attention to this subject.   For example, one of the oldest inter-faith groups, started in Wolverhampton in 1974, held a conference on the subject of Inter-Faith Worship in 1982.   That year there had been a Service of Prayer for Peace and Disarmament organized by the Council of Christian Churches in which there were readings from the Bhagavad Gita and the New Testament, and prayers said by a Sikh, a Muslim and a Christian.   Up to then, however, the Wolverhampton Inter-faith Group had never initiated or organized any inter-faith worship, although they had visited different faiths at worship, as observers, and individuals could participate as far as they felt able.   But as the group had grown closer, they often spoke of praying together, and did share times of silent prayer at the beginning of their meetings.

At this conference reasons given in support of inter-faith worship were that for most faiths in worshipping the One God (albeit by different names), Creator of all, participants share in an expression of a common spirituality, a common search for truth, an inspiration for common action, an affirmation of a common humanity and of common ethical values.

On the other hand, it was recognized that all religious communities should be allowed to clarify and safeguard their own beliefs and convictions about the character and purpose of God and about their own sacred scriptures.

The conference concluded that coming together in worship was not something to be undertaken lightly, but that there was a need for people to prepare themselves to understand others and remove any fear that they will lose anything as a result. People needed to know themselves and each other very well before this stage could be reached.

Subsequent to this conference, Wolverhampton Inter-Faith Group started a United Service of Prayer for Peace which now takes place in January each year.

Worship in One Faith Tradition

The practice of groups being present as visitors at a time of worship according to one faith tradition, in the worship place of that faith, as mentioned by the Wolverhampton Group, had been experienced by several groups.

Many felt that this was the ideal way to start to get to know about the worship of different faith communities, for it gave the opportunity for members to broaden their understanding of and respect for different forms of worship and enabled relationships to be deepened. The host community should make clear to the visitors what might be required of them in the way of dress (covering head, arms and/or legs, removing shoes etc) positions for worship (sitting on floor, standing for long periods, men and women separated etc) and in how much of the words or action they would be welcome to join. This information should be provided prior to the visit to avoid potential embarrassment. Conversely the hosts must accept that certain words or actions might not be acceptable to everyone, and no-one should be made to feel that they must participate when they would prefer to remain as an observer. Moreover, it should be made clear that, although the host faith will be expected to be honest about its beliefs, such occasions should never be allowed to become vehicles for proselytism. It should be clear that their purpose is for education and shared experiences.

If such an experience is followed by social interaction over a cup of tea or fruit juice, or sometimes something more substantial, it can give the opportunity for informal questions, answers and explanations which can further promote understanding and respect between peoples of different faiths. Some groups found that such an experience led naturally into other inter-faith meetings and activities.

The Coventry Inter-Faith Group explained how they made such visits during a Peace Walk, and West Bromwich Inter-Faith Forum have made similar visits during One World Week.

Coming Together to Pray

A lesser number of groups had 'come together to pray' or taken part in consecutive or serial worship where members from participating faiths either contribute to the occasion using their own prayers and/or holy writings, or do in turn what is characteristic of their own worship. Others attending are enabled to share to the extent to which they feel they can conscientiously do so.

Some groups felt that this was a stage further along the road towards spiritual maturity, for it demands greater sensitivity in presenting one's own tradition so as not to give offence to others. As one group put it, 'one must be able to listen to oneself with other's ears'. It was also felt that such an occasion cannot be embarked upon until groups know each other well and feel that they have developed a sense of unity, for there should be no friction, and nothing which might give offence.

Events of this kind encourage co-operation between the different faiths represented to work out a theme and a format which is acceptable to all, with the wording of prayers and the choice of readings carefully considered. The desirability of having a theme was stressed so as to give a unity to the different contributions. Various themes which had been used by the groups were : Peace; Light; Creation/The World/Ecology; Conflict Resolution/Reconciliation; Mediation; Universal Love for All Mankind; Harmony; One Family; Economics; Justice; Pilgrimage; and Sacred Writings. Many of these have been used in compiling the second part of this book which includes readings and prayers chosen by members of different faiths.

However, although it is hoped that these will be useful, they are there only for guidance, and those planning such services may prefer to find other contributions on the agreed theme from their own traditions.

Many groups used the annual One World Week theme while others had found that a specific world event such as the Gulf War or Bosnia had provided the theme and reason for their wish to come together to pray.

Many groups also found visible and tangible symbols, such as light, water, flowers etc a unifying force, useful as a focal point and an aid to meditation.

In some cases the occasion was mainly one of silence broken by contributions of speech and song.   Silence was felt to be a way of overcoming many problems, and engendered a spiritual fellowship.   As one group put it, 'In silence we transcend language'.

It was felt that this form of prayer can be an open and honest attempt to support each other in faith, and some people found that such an experience broadened and deepened their own faith.   Again, others found that such an event was a catalyst which opened people to inter-faith sharing and its spirit.

The organisers of such an occasion should, however, be aware of the danger of it becoming a show piece or a 'performance'.

Such a form of service, with prayers, readings from Holy Books and other writings (e.g. Kahil Gibran), meditation and music according to a theme, had been used by groups during One World Week and the Week of Prayer for World Peace.

Coming to pray together

Fewer groups had 'come to pray together' or hold events with an agreed common order and content in which it was hoped everyone would feel able to participate.   Those groups which had embarked upon such an event said that it was most important to ensure that representatives of all the faith communities involved took part in the planning from the very beginning.   Some groups felt that the very act of preparation, when people of different faiths need to be completely honest with one another, and accept what others have to say in a spirit of learning and humility, created a greater spirit of fellowship.   But the need for very careful planning, consultation and unanimous decisions on such things as form, order and content was stressed, so that the authenticity of each participating faith can be secured.

Reference has been made in the Introduction to the fact that terminology can cause problems for some people, and this is something which should be considered by the planning group. For this reason it may be that some Buddhists who do not believe in a Transcendent Power might feel unable to participate.

Again, the need for a uniting theme, possibly as a result of a current or local situation, was stressed, and also the use of symbols. One group suggested that guided meditation can be acceptable to members of all faiths, and another said that such an events should contribute to both the personal and collective spiritual journey of those attending them.

Practical Points to be Considered

Venue :   Although many people would prefer to be in a place not connected with any particular faith when 'coming together to pray' or 'to pray together', yet a secular venue can cause difficulties for others in establishing a viable setting for worship or in creating a suitable environment. The fact that some people feel they need to sit on the floor, while others prefer chairs; some like to kneel while others would rather stand, should be taken into account. Being able to move about or express their devotion through bodily movements is important for some people, while others need to be still and quiet. In some traditions it is required that the leader/s or holy writings be placed in an elevated position, or it is necessary to face in a particular geographical direction.

These are things which should be discussed in the planning stage so that everyone can accept the arrangements which are eventually made.

Day and Time :   Unless there is good reason to include the ritual of one particular faith community in an inter-faith service, it is usually better to avoid having it at a time when any of the participating communities would normally be having their own principal devotions.

Order and Content :   As the finally agreed order and content of such an event is unlikely to be familiar to many of the participants, it is strongly recommended that, where possible, this should be written (or printed), and include guidance as to what the participants might expect to happen, and what they may be encouraged to do, with alternatives (e.g. stand or sit or kneel) made clear. Those preparing such an event should also ensure that those who are asked to participate know how long should be their contribution.

Language : As some of the readings, prayers or mantras which may be included in such a event are likely to be read or chanted in the language in which they were originally written, it is helpful for everyone to know their meaning in order to help them with their participation. Where possible, translations should be available.

Holy Writings : The treatment, handling and position of the sacred scriptures is an important part of worship within some faith communities, and care should be taken to see that they are duly reverenced and handled only by those authorised so to do.

Symbols and Rituals : Symbols on which people from different faiths can agree can be a helpful and uplifting part of shared worship. Ritual often expresses the beliefs of one particular faith which cannot, in sincerity, be shared by others, and therefore limits participation in them.

Music and Singing : Although an integral part of worship for many faith communities, many Muslims would not wish to sing during a service and some would be hesitant about the use of music. If they are a participating community, they should be consulted on the appropriateness of the arrangements in this respect.

Silence and Meditation : The use of silence and meditation will depend to a large extent on the size and inclinations of the participating group and on the occasion. Long periods of silence would probably be inappropriate during a Civic Service, whereas many inter-faith groups have developed the practice of having a period of silent prayer at the commencement of all their meetings. Those preparing a service should consider how much time should be allowed for silence and for meditation, guided or otherwise, and those leading it should be directed accordingly.

Food and Drink : For many the sharing of food and drink is a continuation of the fellowship engendered by prayer. However, those preparing such refreshment should ascertain that the dietary regulations of different faith communities are catered for, and, if necessary, the foods clearly labelled so that their contents are known. Similarly, bottled water or fruit juices should be provided for those who do not drink tea, coffee or alcoholic beverages.

THE ANTHOLOGY

The Anthology

Key to Symbols used in Anthology

 Islam
Crescent moon and a
star

 Baha'i Faith
Nine pointed star
symbolizes belief that
all religions are divine

 Hinduism
The sacred sound 'Om'
used in prayers

 Sikhism
Symbol known as Ek-
Onkar which represents
righteousness and truth

 Judaism
Star of David

 Buddhism
Represents the wheel of
the Dhamma - Buddha's
teaching

 Jainism
A hand containing a
wheel signifying rebirth

 Zoroastrianism
Denotes the sacred fire
which represents
righteousness and truth

 Christianity
Represents the death of
Jesus, who then rose
again

Communities in Unity

 It is sweet to have friends in need: and to share enjoyment is sweet.

(Dhammapada)

 May you be drawn together in friendship and may extraordinary development make brotherhood a reality and truth.

(Foundations of World Unity)

 Who to consider the true community of faith ?
Where there is discourse about the one God
We are commanded to worship one God.
Nanak, the true Guru has solved this mystery.

(Adi Granth)

 O mankind! behold, we have created you all out of a male and female, and have made you into nations and tribes, so that you might come to know one another. Verily, the noblest among you in the sight of God is the one who is most deeply conscious of Him.

(Holy Qur'an)

 I pray to Thee, O Lord of Wisdom, and wish that want of faith and evil intention may remain away from Thy flock. Also, I wish that perverse thought and obstinacy may be kept away from the self-reliant; deceit and enmity from the near relatives; slanderers and blamers from friends; and the wicked and deceitful leaders from the world.

(Yasna)

 If God had so willed, He could surely have made you all one single community; but [He willed otherwise] to test you by means of what He has vouchsafed unto you. Vie, then, with one another in doing good works. Unto God you must all return; and then He will make you truly understand all that on which you were wont to differ.

(Holy Qu'ran)

 Love is productive of all right actions. It leads a Christian into an earnest and steady discharge of all social offices, of whatever is due to relations of every kind; to his friends, to his country and to any particular community whereof he is a member. It prevents his willingly hurting or grieving any man. It guides him into a uniform practice of justice and mercy, equally extensive with the principle whence it flows. It constrains him to do all possible good, of every possible kind, to all men; and makes him invariably resolved in every circumstance of life to do that, and that only, to others, which supposing he were himself in the same situation, he would desire they should do to him.

(John Wesley)

The purpose of consultation is to show that the views of several individuals are assuredly preferable to one man, even as the power of a number of men is of course greater than the power of one man. Thus consultation is acceptable in the presence of the Almighty, and hath been enjoined upon the believers, so that they may confer upon ordinary and personal matters, as well as on affairs which are general in nature and universal.

(From a letter of Shoghi Effendi)

Let us pray in our hearts for a League of Souls and a United World. Though we may seem divided by race, creed, colour, class and political prejudices, still, as children of the one God we are able in our souls to feel brotherhood and world unity.   May we work for the creation of a United World in which every nation will be a useful part, guided by God through man's enlightened conscience.
In our hearts we can all learn to be free from hate and selfishness.   Let us pray for harmony among the nations, that they march hand in hand through the gate of a fair new civilization.

(Paramahansa Yogananda)

O God,
Let us be united;
Let us speak in harmony;
Let our minds apprehend alike.
Common be our prayer;
Common be the end of our assembly;
Common be our resolution;
Common be our deliberations.
Alike be our feelings;
Unified be our hearts;
Common be our intentions;
Perfect be our unity.

(Vedas)

Now there are varieties of gifts, but the same Spirit; and there are varieties of services, but the same Lord; and there are varieties of activities, but it is the same God who activates all of them in everyone. To each is given the manifestation of the Spirit for the common good. For just as the body is one and has many members, and all the members of the body, though many, are one body, so it is with Christ.   For in the one Spirit we were all baptised into one body - Jews or Greeks, slaves or free - and we were all made to drink of one Spirit.

(The New Testament)

Compassion

The Lord is good to all; he has compassion on all he has made.

(From a Song of David in the Psalms)

God does not burden any human being with more than he is well able to bear.

(Holy Qu'ran)

Whatever you did for one of the least of these brothers of mine, you did it for me.

(The New Testament)

Have contentment in your mind,
And compassion towards all beings.

(Adi Granth)

Seek to do brave and lovely things that are left undone by the majority of people. Give gifts of love and peace to those whom others pass by.

(Parmahansa Yogananda)

Beware lest ye offend any heart, lest ye speak against any one in his absence, lest ye estrange yourselves from the servants of God. You must consider all His servants as your own family and relations. Direct your whole effort towards the happiness of those who are despondent, bestow food upon the hungry, clothe the needy and glorify the humble. Be a helper to every helpless one, and manifest kindness to your fellow creatures in order that you may attain the good pleasure of God.

('Abdu'l-Baha: The Promulgation of Universal Peace)

Here is thy footstool and there rest thy feet where live the poorest, and lowliest, and lost.
When I try to bow to thee, my obeisance cannot reach down to the depth where thy feet rest among the poorest, and lowliest, and lost.
Pride can never approach to where thou walkest in the clothes of the humble among the poorest, the lowliest, and lost.
My heart can never find its way to where thou keepest company with the companionless among the poorest, the lowliest, and the lost.

(Rabindranath Tagore)

I will give you a talisman.   Whenever you are in doubt, or when the self becomes too much with you, try the following expedient:
Recall the face of the poorest and the most helpless man whom you may have seen and ask yourself if the step you contemplate is going to be of any use to him.   Will he be able to gain anything by it?   Will it restore him to a control over his own life and destiny?   Then you will find your doubts and your self melting away.

(Gandhi)

From every race and land,
the victims of our day,
abused and hurt by human hands,
are wounded on life's way.

The priest and levite pass
and find no time to wait.
The pressing claims of living call;
they leave them to their fate.

But one of different faith
to care he felt compelled.
His active love like Jesus' own
uplifted, healed and held.

May this example lead
inspire and teach us all
that we may find in others' faith
the God on whom we call.

(Hymn of the Good Samaritan by Andrew Lunn)

Sariputta, one of the Buddha's chief disciples, taught that the development of compassion was a way to remove hostility towards others.   He said, 'Friends, it is like this.   An ill, suffering, very sick person is on a long road.   There are villages far off in front and behind him.   He has no suitable food, suitable medicine, suitable servant, nor a guide to the village.   Another person on the long road might see and establish simple compassion, tender care, and sympathy for that sick person with the thought:
May this person obtain suitable food, suitable medicine, a suitable servant, and a guide to the village.   Why?   So that this person may be free from misfortune and misery at this time.'

Sariputta continues, 'Friends, it is similar with regard to an individual with impure physical and verbal activities who does not obtain openness of mind and clarity of mind from time to time.   Friends, simple compassion, tender care, and sympathy should be established with regard to such an individual by means of the thought:
May this respectable individual abandon improper physical activities and cultivate proper ones.   May he abandon improper verbal activities and cultivate proper ones.   Why?   So that this respectable individual will not be reborn in a state of loss, in a bad fate, in ruin, or in hell after dissolution of the body after death.
In this way hostility is eliminated with regard to that individual'.

(Anguttara-nikaya)

Forgiveness & Reconciliation

Countless wrongs does the son,
Forgives and remembers none, his mum.

(Adi Granth)

Forgive us our trespasses, as we forgive them that trespass against us.

(The New Testament)

Then came Peter, and said to him, Lord, how oft shall my brother sin against me, and I forgive him?   Until seven times?   Jesus saith unto him, I say not unto thee, Until seven times; but, Until seventy times seven.

(The New Testament)

If a wise one knowingly or unknowingly commits any sinful act, then on realising his mistake he immediately repents and takes more care in all his normal duties.

(Dasvaikalika Sutra)

As a child intentionally or unintentionally
Commits many bad deeds
The father tells off, scolds
Then teaches and explains in many ways
Then holds and embraces the child
In the same way, the Lord blesses and forgives past sins
And shows the right way.

(Adi Granth)

Were it not for the grace and mercy of Allah on you, and that Allah is full of kindness and mercy, Ye would be ruined indeed.
Let not those among you who are endued with grace and amplitude of means resolve by oath against helping their kinsmen, those in want, and those who have left their homes in Allah's cause: Let them forgive and overlook.   Do you not wish that Allah should forgive you?   For Allah is oft-forgiving and merciful.

(The Holy Qur'an)

Praise the Lord, O my soul;
all my inmost being, praise his holy name.
Praise the Lord, O my soul,
and forget not all his benefits -
who forgives all your sins
and heals all your diseases,
who redeems your life from the pit
and crowns you with love and compassion,
who satisfies your desires with good things
so that your youth is renewed like the eagle's.

(A Psalm of David)

In the company of saints and holy people.
No more the feeling of us and them
No one an enemy, none a stranger
I am a friend of all.

(Adi Granth)

Hate is not conquered by hate: hate is conquered by love.

(Dhammapada)

Do not allow difference of opinion, or diversity of thought to separate you
from your fellow-men, or to be the cause of dispute, hatred and strife in
your hearts.

('Abdu'l I-Baha: Paris Talks)

Overcome anger by peacefulness; overcome evil by good.
Overcome the mean by generosity; and the man who lies by truth.

(Dhammapada)

The good deed and the evil deed are not alike. Repel the evil deed with
one that is better. Then lo! he between whom and thee there was
enmity will become as though he was a bosom friend.

(The Holy Qur'an)

If any differences arise amongst you, behold Me standing before your
face, and overlook the faults of one another for My name's sake, and as a
token of your love for My manifest and resplendent Cause.

(Gleanings from the Writings of Baha'u'llah)

Theories only lead to fighting; thus the name of God which ought to bring
peace has been the cause of half the bloodshed of the world. Go direct
to the source. Ask God what He is. Unless He answers, He is not. But
every religion teaches that He does answer.

(Swami Vivekananda)

Let the ugliness of unkindness in others compel me to make myself
beautiful with loving-kindness.
May harsh speech from my companions remind me to use sweet words
always.
If stones from evil minds are cast at me, let me send in return only
missiles of goodwill.
As a jasmine vine sheds its flowers over the hands delivering axe blows at
its roots, so, on all who act inimically towards me may I shower the
blossoms of forgiveness.

(Paramahansa Yogananda)

Forgive us, Lord, our selfishness that spurns your burning love;
O'erlook our spiritual weakness that's afraid the world to move.
Brace us for supreme adventure that is fuelled from above
By the power that the Spirit prompts.

(Frank Whaling)

Freedom and Justice

A wise man calmly considers what is right and what is wrong and faces
different opinions with truth, non-violence and peace.
This man is guarded by truth and is a guardian of truth.

(Dhammapada)

Be vigilant, that ye may not do injustice to any one, be it to the extent of
a grain of mustard seed. Tread ye the path of justice, for this, verily, is
the straight path.

(Gleanings from the writings of Baha'u'llah)

Allah commands justice, the doing of good and liberality to kith and kin,
and he forbids all shameful deeds, and injustice and rebellion, he instructs
you, that ye may receive admonition.

(The Holy Qur'an)

Good and bad deeds will be narrated before the God of Justice
Some will be brought in closer to God,
Others pushed away on the basis of their action.
Those who have prayed and meditated, toiled appropriately
Leave this world with radiant faces
And many more will be emancipated with them.

(Adi Granth)

If ye, O Mortals, realize and understand the laws of happiness and pain
ordained by Mazda; and if you learn that liars and wicked persons shall
face age long punishment but pious and righteous ones shall enjoy everlasting prosperity, then you shall reach real contentment and salvation, by
learning this principle.

(Yasna)

The sinner and deluded man may succeed at first and even attain high
renown for his evil deeds, but Ye, O Lord of Life, are well aware of
everything and shall judge the deeds of everyone from his or her own
motives through Thy Wisdom. O Mazda [Lord of Wisdom] at last
wherever Thy Rule extends, the Eternal Law of Truth shall prevail.

(Yasna)

O you who have attained to faith: be ever steadfast in your devotion to
God, bearing witness to the truth in all equity; and never let hatred of
anyone lead you into the sin of deviating from justice. Be just: this is
closest to being God-conscious. And remain conscious of God; verily,
God is aware of all that you do.

(The Holy Qur'an)

Creator! you are the same creator of all equally.
If the strong attacks the other equally strong
Then there is no complaint, no grievance.
But when a fierce tiger preys on helpless cattle
Then the shepherd must explain!

(Adi Granth)

O God, we pray for all those in our world who are suffering from injustice:
For those who are discriminated against because of their race, colour or religion;
For those imprisoned for working for the relief of oppression;
For those who are hounded for speaking the inconvenient truth;
For those tempted to violence as a cry against overwhelming hardship;
For those deprived of reasonable health and education;
For those suffering from hunger and famine;
For those too weak to help themselves and who have no-one else to help them;
For the unemployed who cry out for work but do not find it.
We pray for anyone of our acquaintance who is personally affected by injustice.
Forgive us, Lord, if we unwittingly share in the conditions or in a system that perpetuates injustice.
Show us how we can serve your children and make your love practical by washing their feet.

(Mother Teresa)

Where the mind is without fear and the head is held high;
Where knowledge is free;
Where the world has not been broken up into fragments by narrow domestic walls;
Where words come out from the depth of truth;
Where tireless striving stretches its arms towards perfection;
Where the clear stream of reason has not lost its way into the dreary desert sand of dead habit;
Where the mind is led forward by thee into ever-widening thought and action -
Into that heaven of freedom my Father, let me awake.

(Rabindranath Tagore)

For the healing of the nations,
Lord, we pray with one accord;
for a just and equal sharing
of the things that earth affords
To a life of love in action
help us rise and pledge our word...

All that kills abundant living,
let it from the earth be banned;
pride of status, race or schooling,
dogmas that obscure your plan.
In our common quest for justice
may we hallow life's brief span...
See also p.113 for verse 2
(Fred Kaan)
© 1968 Stainer and Bell Ltd, London, England

Listen, Lord! Hear my prayer for justice!
Listen to my plea.
Hear my prayer,
For my lips do not deceive.
My Judgment comes from You,
For Your eyes see what is right.

(A prayer of David from The Psalms)

Healing

The hunger of passions is the greatest disease.   Disharmony is the greatest sorrow.

(Dhammapada)

Now may every living thing feeble or strong, omitting none, tall or middle aged or short, supple or gross of form, seen or unseen, dwelling near or far, born or yet unborn, may every living thing be full of bliss.

(The Buddha)

He came to me in anguished hunger;
And I raised him up and fed him.

He came to me with bleeding sores,
Lamenting, wailing, sobbing much;
And I nursed his wounds and soothed his many hurts.

She came to me in great turmoil, Frenzied, fearful, bubbling over
With all the agony
Of this troubled world,
Her eyes imprisoned in the dust;
And I cleansed her eyes and healed her vision.

The small child came,
Stumbling, frightened, sick in heart,
Bewildered by the evil
Which filled her universe with raucous discord;
And I taught her the music of the celestial spheres.

They came, and came, and came -
The broken, the helpless, the spiritually lost,
In infinite numbers they came.

(Source unknown)

God does not let His servant suffer a difficult hour
Such is his prerogative
God puts His healing Hand upon His people
Sustains them in every breath
I am attached to the Lord
Saviour in the beginning,
Saviour at the end and always.

(Adi Granth)

There are two ways of healing sickness, material means and spiritual means.   The first is by the use of remedies, of medicines; the second consists in praying to God and in turning to Him.   Both means should be used and practised.

Now, if thou wishest to know the Divine remedy which will heal man from all sickness and will give him the health of the Divine Kingdom, know that it is the precepts and teachings of God.   Guard them sacredly.

(Baha'i World Faith)

The knowledge of the healing art is the most important of all the sciences, for it is the greatest means from God, the Life-giver, for preserving the bodies of all people, and He has put it in the forefront of all sciences and wisdoms.

Say: Thy Name is my healing, O my God, and remembrance of Thee is my remedy. Nearness to Thee is my hope, and love for Thee is my companion. Thy mercy to me is my healing and my succour in both this world and the world to come. Thou, verily, art the All-Bountiful, the All-Knowing, the All-Wise.

(Baha'u'llah and the New Era)

Peace has come, the Lord has caused it,
High fever and sins have gone, my brother,
Repeat the Lord's name daily with your tongue,
Reflect on the qualities of the unfathomable Lord,
In the company of the righteous salvation is obtained,
Sing the praises of the pure regularly every day,
Your suffering cease and be saved, my friend
Concentrate your mind. Remember God with word and deed.

(Adi Granth)

O Spirit, teach us to heal the body by recharging it with Thy cosmic energy, to heal the mind by concentration and cheerfulness, and to heal the disease of soul-ignorance by the divine medicine of meditation on Thee.

(Paramahansa Yogananda)

Heavenly Father, teach me to remember Thee in poverty or prosperity, in sickness or health, in ignorance or wisdom. May I open my closed eyes of unbelief and behold Thine instantaneously healing light.

(Paramahansa Yogananda)

O Allah! Give me light and purity, and preserve me from all disease, sickness, calamity or corruption, and also through this washing purify my heart, my body, my bones, flesh and blood, my hair and skin, my brain and nerves and every place I touch the earth, and provide me with a witness on the day of my poverty, necessity and requirement.

(Said during the Pilgrimage of Hajj)

Heal us, Lord, and we shall be healed; save us, and we shall be saved; for it is You we praise. Send relief and healing for all our diseases, our sufferings and our wounds; for You are a merciful and faithful healer. Blessed are you, Lord, who heals the sick.

(Jewish Service Book)

Human Dignity

A poor person's mouth is God's treasure chest.

(A Sikh saying)

He who knows doubts [understands the instability] knows life.
He who does not know doubts [does not understand this instability] does
not know life.
The wise ones are those who maintain stability of mind, follow the path
of non-violence and truth.

(Acharanga Sutra)

Have We not opened thy heart, and lifted from thee the burden that had
weighed so heavily on thy back? and raised thee high in dignity?

(Holy Qur'an)

Even as a mother protects with her life her child, her only child, so with a
boundless heart should one cherish all living beings.

(Sutta-Nipata)

Our conscience goads us daily at our fellows' poverty;
Injustice, war and cruelty are there for all to see.
Where lies the driving motive that will make all humans free?
In our world where the Spirit prompts.

We would hand in hand with others march in concert with the throng
Out of every creed and nation working for a planet strong
In the century that beckons - Oh!   Beat now the starting gong!
To the sound that the Spirit prompts.

(Frank Whaling)

The truthful person, though of small possessions and poor should be loved
and respected, but followers of untruth, though of great possessions and
power should be despised and regarded as wicked.

(Yasna)

The true believers are those whose hearts are filled with awe at the
mention of Allah, and whose faith grows stronger as they listen to His
revelations.   They are those who put their trust in the Lord, pray
steadfastly, and bestow in alms of that which We have given them.
Such are the true believers.   They shall be exalted and forgiven by their
Lord, and a generous provision shall be made for them.

(Holy Qur'an)

My heart praises the Lord;
my soul is glad because of God my Saviour
His name is holy;
from one generation to another he shows mercy to those who honour
him.
He has stretched out his mighty arm
and scattered the proud with all their plans.
He has brought down mighty kings from their thrones,
and lifted up the lowly.
He has filled the hungry with good things,
and sent the rich away with empty hands.

(The New Testament)

O Son of Being! Thou art My lamp and My light is in thee. Get thou
from it thy radiance and seek none other than Me. For I have created
thee rich and have bountifully shed my favour upon thee.

O son of Being! With the hands of power I made thee and with the
fingers of strength I created thee; and within thee have I placed the
essence of My light. Be thou content with it and seek naught else, for
My work is perfect and My command is binding. Question it not, nor
have a doubt thereof.

O son of Spirit! I created thee rich, why dost thou bring thyself down to
poverty? Noble I made thee, wherewith dost thou abase thyself? Out
of the essence of knowledge I gave thee being, why seekest thou
enlightenment from anyone beside Me? Out of the clay of love I moulded
thee, how dost thou busy thyself with another? Turn thy sight unto
thyself, that thou mayest find Me standing within thee, mighty, powerful,
and self-subsisting.

(Baha'u'llah, The Hidden Words)

I have bled for Thy Name; and for Thy Name's sake I am willing ever to
bleed. Like a mighty warrior, with gory limbs, injured body, wounded
honour, and a thorn crown of derision, undismayed I fight on. My scars I
wear as roses of courage, of inspiration to persevere in the battle against
evil.
I may continue to suffer blows on my arms outstretched to help others,
and receive persecution instead of love, but my soul shall ever bask in the
sunshine of Thy blessings, O Lord.

(Paramhansa Yogananda)

Our World

God says,
I am the wind that breathes upon the sea.
I am the wave on the ocean,
I am the murmur of the leaves rustling
I am the power of the trees growing,
I am the bud breaking into blossom,
I am the child running in the street,
I am the woman working in the factory,
I am the poor seeking justice,
I am the cry of broken nature,
I am the movement of the salmon swimming,
I am the courage of the wild boar fighting,
I am the strength of people organising,
I am the hope that rises in their hearts,
I am the strength of the ox pulling the plough,
I am the size of the mighty oak,
I am the thoughts of all people
Who praise my beauty and grace.

(Based on an ancient Welsh prayer)

Him the sun cannot express, nor the moon, nor the stars; this lightening
cannot express Him, nor what we speak of as fire. Through Him do they
all shine.

(Upanishad)

Blessed be God who did not let the world lack anything,
who created for it beautiful creatures,
and these beautiful trees,
that we may see them and be filled with joy.

(Talmud. Berakhot)

Nature we see
Nature we hear
Nature we observe with awe, wonder and joy
Nature in the skies
Nature in the whole creation
Nature in the sacred texts
Nature in all reflection
Nature in food, in water, in clothes and in love for all
Nature in species, kinds and colours
Nature in life-forms
Nature in good deeds
Nature in pride and ego
Nature in air, water and fire
Nature in the soil of the earth.
All nature is yours, O powerful Creator
You command it, observe it and pervade within it.

(Adi Granth)

It is God who has raised the heavens without any supports that you could see, and is established on the throne of His almightiness; and He has made the sun and the moon subservient to His laws, each running its course for a term.

And it is He who has spread the earth wide and placed upon it firm mountains and running waters, and created thereon two sexes of every kind of plant; and He who causes the night to cover the day.

Verily, in all this there are messages indeed for people who think.

And there are on earth tracts of land close by one another,

with vineyards, and fields of grain, and date palms growing in clusters from one room or standing alone all watered with the same water; and yet, some of them have We favoured above others by way of the food which they provide.

Verily, in all this there are messages indeed for people who use their reason.

(The Holy Qur'an)

How all-encompassing are the wonders of His boundless grace! Behold how they have pervaded the whole of creation.   Such is their virtue that not a single atom in the entire universe can be found that does not declare the evidence of His might, which doth not glorify His holy Name, or is not expressive of the effulgent light of His unity.   So perfect and comprehensive is His creation that no mind nor heart, however keen or pure, can ever grasp the nature of the most insignificant of His creatures;   much less fathom the mystery of Him Who is the Day Star of Truth, Who is the invisible and unknowable Essence.

(Gleanings from the Writings of Baha'u'llah)

The whole universe is ever in his power.   He is pure consciousness, the creator of time: all-powerful, all-knowing.   It is under his rule that the work of creation revolves in its evolution, and we have earth, and water, and ether, and fire and air.

His being is the source of all being, the seed of all things that in this life have their life.   He is beyond time and space, and yet he is the God of infinite forms who dwells in our inmost thoughts, and who is seen by those who love him.

May God who is hidden in nature, even as the silkworm is hidden in the web of silk he made, lead us to unison with his own Spirit.

(Svetasvatara Upanishad)

As our body is born, plants are born, as we grow so plants grow, as we have reason [mind] so plants have reason, as our body is damaged when cut so a plant is damaged when cut; as we need food so plants need food, as we are mortal so plants are mortal, as we have ups and downs plants have ups and downs.

As we have some irregularities [in our life] so plants have some irregularities.

(Acharanga Sutra)

You are master of the earth, O human
Responsible for all life-forms.

(Adi Granth)

Love all God's creation - the whole of it.   Every grain of sand.
Love every leaf, every ray of light.   Love the animals, love the plants,
love everything.   If you love everything you will perceive the mystery of
God in all.   Once you perceive this you will begin to understand it better
every day and you will come at last to love the whole world with an all-
embracing love.

(Dostoevsky)

The planters of groves and fruitful trees,
And they who build causeways and dams,
And wells construct, and watering-sheds,
And [to the homeless] shelter give:
Of such as these, by day, by night,
Forever merit give.

(The Buddha: Samvutta-Nikaya)

Chaos and confusion are daily increasing in the world.   They will attain
such intensity as to render the frame of mankind unable to bear them.
Then will men be awakened and become aware that religion is the
impregnable stronghold and the manifest light of the world, and its laws,
exhortations and teachings and the source of life on earth.

(Words of 'Abdu'l-Baha)

O, Thou, Creator of Our Mother Earth, the Water and the Plants, O
Mazda, grant me Eternal Perfection, through Thy most Holy Spirit.   Do
grant me strength and stability, O My Lord, and reveal to me the Lord's
teachings.

(Yasna)

Blessed art thou, O Lord our God, King of the Universe, who has made the
world lacking in naught, but has produced therein goodly trees wherewith
to give delight unto the children of men.   Blessed art thou, who has given
the wisdom of thy hands to flesh and blood, that beautiful cities might
rise to thy glory.   Blessed art thou, who has created joy and gladness,
mirth and exultation, pleasure and delight, love, brotherhood, peace and
fellowship, O Lord our God, King of the Universe.

(A Hebrew Prayer)

We thank you, Lord, for all the ways in which you have shown yourself to
us.
We thank you for your presence in nature: for the song of a bird, the lilt
of a mountain, the colour of a flower, the joy of animals with their young.
We thank you for your coming through other humans; for the laughter of
children, the care of mothers, the love of families, the concern of
neighbours, the thoughtfulness of friends.
We thank you for coming to us in the small things of life: for washing up,
for lessons, for leisure, for imagination, for play.
We thank you for the kingdom of God within us.

(Frank Whaling)

Hey man!   Everything belongs to God.   And don't you dare go round
abusing it.
For you are responsible and accountable for all that has been created.
(New version of Psalm 24 written by young people at an Environmental
Workcamp in 1991)

Peace

May men and women helped by just leaders and kings enjoy peace and rest in their own clans and villages.

(Yasna)

In the light of his understanding he has found his freedom: his thoughts are peace, his words are peace and his work is peace.

(Dhammapada)

Awake in peace, sit in peace
Understand this message, leave fear and be serene
The Saviour is our one Lord.
Sleep without fear, awake without fear
Everywhere you are present O Lord
Peace at home and peace outdoors.

(Adi Granth)

It is He who sent down tranquillity [peace] into the hearts of the Believers, that they may add faith to their faith, for to Allah belong the forces of the heavens and the earth; and Allah is full of knowledge and wisdom.

(The Holy Qur'an)

Peace is found through surrender to good, through devotion.
People who are loving, who practice stillness, and who delight in meditation and good actions, are really peaceful. Peace is the altar of God, the condition in which happiness exists.

(Paramahansa Yogananda)

The bulk of humanity now realiseth what a great calamity war is and how war turneth man into a ferocious animal, causing prosperous cities and villages to be reduced to ruins and the foundations of the human edifice to crumble. Now since all men have been awakened and their ears are attentive, it is time for the promulgation of universal peace - a peace based on righteousness and justice, that mankind may not be exposed to further dangers in the future. Now is the dawn of universal peace, and the first streaks of its light are beginning to appear. We earnestly hope that its effulgent orb may shine forth and flood the east and the west with its radiance.

('Abdu'l-Baha: Peace)

If they [your enemies] incline to peace, incline thou to it as well, and place thy trust in God; verily, He alone is all-hearing, all knowing.

(The Holy Qur'an)

Let no one give ear to the words of the false and wicked one because such persons shall lead the home, the village, the town and the country to ruin and destruction. It is, therefore, our duty to resist such persons and repel them with spiritual weapons of purity and righteousness.

(Yasna)

O Man!   The one you are thinking of killing is [no one but] yourself.   The one you are ordering about is yourself.   The one you are thinking of putting in misery is yourself.   The one you are thinking of catching is yourself.   Think of this.   With this sort of understanding you will have equality [Friendship] with all living beings.   Knowing that everyone has to bear the fruits of his own deeds, one should not kill any living beings.

(Acharanga Sutra)

May there be peace in the higher regions; may there be peace in the firmament; may there be peace on earth.   May the waters flow peacefully; may the herbs and plants grow peacefully; may all the living powers bring unto us peace.   The supreme Lord is peace.   May we all be in peace, peace and only peace; and may that peace come unto each of us.   Shant, shanti, shanti.

(Vedas)

We ask that we live and labour in peace,
Each man shall be our neighbour in peace,
Distrust and hatred shall turn to love,
All the prisoners freed,
And our only war will be the one
Against all human need.

(Donald Swann)

Eternal God
Eternal Ruler
who makes peace and creates all things;
Help all of us, that we may ever adhere to the concept of peace,
so that true and abundant peace prevail between man and man, between husband and wife,
and no strife separate humanity even in thought.
You make peace in your heavens, you bring contrary elements harmoniously together:
Extend abundant peace to us and to the whole world,
so that all discords be resolved in great love and peace and with one mind and one heart all come near to you and your law in truth,
and all form one union to do your will with a whole heart.
Eternal God of peace, bless us with peace.

(Nahman of Bratzlav)

Lord, make me an instrument of Thy peace.
Where there is hatred, let me sow love
Where there is injury, pardon.
Where there is doubt, faith.
Where there is despair, hope.
Where there is darkness, light.
Where there is sadness, joy.
O Divine Master, grant that I may not so much seek to be consoled as to console;
to be understood, as to understand;
to be loved, as to love;
for it is in giving that we receive,
it is in pardoning that we are pardoned,
and it is in dying that we are born to Eternal Life.

(St. Francis of Assisi)

Relationships

You are my father, you are my mother.
You are my relative, you are my brother.
You are my saviour everywhere,
So why and from whom shall I be afraid?

(Adi Granth)

O mankind: be conscious of your Lord and Sustainer, who has created you out of one living entity, and out of it created its mate, and out of the two spread abroad a multitude of men and women. And remain conscious of God, in whose name you demand your rights from one another, and of these ties of kinship.

(The Holy Qur'an)

I recognised Thee, O Mazda Ahura, as pure and holy when good thoughts entered my mind and asked me, Who art Thou; To which family do Thou belong? Which path would you choose when you are in doubt? The path which leads to the benefit of your brothers and relatives, or the one which is to your own benefit?

(Yasna)

In five ways a member of a family should minister to his friends and companions: by generosity; by courtesy; by benevolence; by equality, treating them as he treats himself; and by being true to his word.
Thus ministered to, his friends and companions love him in these five ways: they protect him when he is in need of protection; they look after his property when he is unable to; they become a refuge in danger; they do not forsake him in his troubles; and they respect even others related to him.

(Digha-Nikaya)

A wise one shows proper courtesy towards the elderly and the learned ones. His mind is always as stable as the pole-star, his senses and feelings of attachment are always under control, and he is always equipped with the virtues of self-control and penance.

(Dasvaikalika Sutra)

Do not be satisfied until each one with whom you are concerned is to you like a member of your family. Regard each one either as a father, a brother, or as a sister, or as a mother, or as a child. If you can attain to this, your difficulties will vanish; you will know what to do.

(Abdu'l-Baha)

He who befriends you, befriends Allah, he who antagonises you, antagonises Allah, he who loves you, loves Allah, he who holds fast to you, holds fast to Allah.

(The Holy Qur'an)

I will behold the Invisible in the visible forms of my father, mother and friends, sent here to love and help me. I will show my love for God by loving them all. In their human expressions of affection, I will recognise only the One Divine Love.

(Paramahansa Yogananda)

Be it thy will, O Eternal God,
to cause us to dwell in love, companionship, peace, and friendship;
to widen our boundaries through disciples,
to prosper our goal with hope and with future,
to appoint us a share in the Garden of Eden,
to direct us in thy world through good companions and good impulse,
that we may rise in the morning and find
our heart waiting to fear thy name.

(Talmud)

This is my prayer to thee, my Lord, strike at the root of penury in my heart, give me the strength lightly to bear my joys and sorrows; give me the strength to make my love fruitful in service; give me the strength never to disown the poor or bend my knees before insolent might; give me the strength to raise my mind above daily trifles and give me the strength to surrender my strength to thy will, with love.

(Rabindranath Tagore)

Our loving Father, help us to remember thee always, as the God of our family, as the bond of our union, as our Protector and Guide, and as our Master whose holy will we are to do in all our actions.   Fill our hearts with love and enable us to give to everyone the love, reverence and tenderness that are due to him or her.   May we love and honour our parents in heart, word and deed, treat our brothers and sisters with uniform kindness and tenderness.   May husband and wife be ever true to their holy union and may parents set an example of kind and holy behaviour to their children.   Enable us all to bear patiently with the defects and shortcomings of one another, to serve one another, and help one another in difficulties, and keep us free from anger and selfishness. Give us strength to do our allotted duties faithfully and enable us to realise, by living sweet and holy lives, the ideal of a happy and blessed home.

(Brahmo Samaj)

Remembering that God is love, a Christian is conformed to the same likeness.   He is full of love to his neighbour: of universal love, not confined to one sect or party, not restrained to those who agree with him in opinions, or in outward modes of worship, or to those who are allied to him by blood or recommended by nearness of place.   Neither does he love those only that love him, or that are endeared to him by intimacy of acquaintance.   But his love resembles that of him whose mercy is over all his works.   It soars above all these scanty bonds, embracing neighbours and strangers, friends and enemies; yes, not only the good and gentle but also the froward, the evil and unthankful.   For he loves every soul that God has made, every child of man, of whatever place or nation.

(John Wesley)

Together in Times of Trouble

Verily, those who have attained to faith, as well as those who follow the Jewish faith, and the Christians, and the Sabians - all who believe in God and the Last Day and do righteous deeds - shall have their reward with their Sustainer; and no fear need they have, and neither shall they grieve.

(The Holy Qur'an)

Hurt not with the body, but use your body well.
Hurt not with words, but use your words well.
Hurt not with the mind, but use your mind well.
O let us live in joy, although having nothing.
In joy let us live like spirits of light.

(Dhammapada)

Teach us, good Lord, to serve the needs of others;
Help us to give and not to count the cost;
Unite us all, for we are born as brothers;
Defeat our Babel with your Pentecost.

(Fred Kaan)

What profit is there in agreeing that universal friendship is good, and talking of the solidarity of the human race as a grand ideal? Unless these thoughts are translated into the world of action, they are useless. The wrong in the world continues to exist just because people talk only of their ideals, and do not strive to put them into practice. If actions took the place of words, the world's misery would very soon be changed into comfort.

('Abdu'l-Baha)

O ye beloved of the Lord! In this sacred Dispensation, conflict and contention are in no wise permitted. Every aggressor deprives himself of God's grace. It is incumbent upon everyone to show the utmost love, rectitude of conduct, straightforwardness and sincere kindliness unto all the peoples and kindreds of the world, be they friends or strangers. So intense must be the spirit of love and loving-kindness, that the stranger may find himself a friend, the enemy a true brother, no difference whatsoever existing between them.

(Baha'i World Faith)

The Lord is the strength of the weak
Eternal, unborn, undying is the Lord.
Revealed as true through the Guru's word.
When one is weakened with pangs of hunger and poverty,
No money and none to give consolation
None to offer help and all work comes to nothing,
Remember the Supreme Lord and gain the everlasting kingdom.

(Adi Granth)

In many ways God saves,
From diseases, sorrows and water dangers.
Countless foes may aim to wound
Yet none may touch the body
If God protects us as his own, sins cannot touch us.
Why talk of anything else
When God protects even in the womb?

(Dasam Granth)

God of our strength, in our weakness help us; in our sorrow comfort us;
in our confusion guide us. Without You our lives are nothing; with You
there is fullness of life for evermore.

(Jewish Service Book)

When I needed a neighbour were you there, were you there?
When I needed a neighbour were you there?
And the creed and the colour and the name won't matter,
Were you there?

I was hungry and thirsty, were you there, were you there?
I was hungry and thirsty, were you there?
And the creed and the colour and the name won't matter,
Were you there?

I was cold, I was naked, were you there, were you there?
I was cold, I was naked, were you there?
And the creed and the colour and the name won't matter,
Were you there?

When I needed a shelter were you there, were you there?
When I needed a shelter were you there?
And the creed and the colour and the name won't matter,
Were you there?

When I needed a healer were you there, were you there?
When I needed a healer were you there?
And the creed and the colour and the name won't matter,
Were you there?

Wherever you travel I'll be there, I'll be there.
Wherever you travel I'll be there.
And the creed and the colour and the name won't matter,
I'll be there.

(Sydney Carter)
© 1968 and 1973 Stainer and Bell Ltd, London, England.

Tolerance

In the estimation of God all men are equal. There is no distinction or preference for any soul, in the realm of His justice and equity.
God did not make these divisions; these divisions have their origin in man himself. Therefore, as they are against the plan and purpose of God they are false and imaginary.
This variety in forms and colouring, which is manifest in all the kingdoms, is according to creative wisdom and hath a divine purpose.
The diversity in the human family should be the cause of love and harmony, as it is in music where many different notes blend together in the making of a perfect chord.

('Abdu'l-Baha: The Advent of Divine Justice)

There is no coercion in matters of faith

(The Holy Qur'an)

Temple and the mosque are the same,
Hindu worship and Muslim prayer the same,
All humans are one,
Our misunderstanding creates difference.

(Dasam Granth)

If my Hindu, Buddhist or Muslim neighbour is as much a child of God as I am, and if nothing that either of us does to reach or know God can fall outside the mercy and the providence of God, then we are indeed brothers and sisters. We are pilgrims, not strangers. We have much to learn from each other. We belong together to God, our common creator.

(Wesley Ariarajah)

One should not honour only one's own religion and condemn the religions of others, but one should honour others' religions too. So doing, one helps one's own religion to grow and render service to the religions of others too. In acting otherwise one depraves one's own religion and also does harm to other religions. Whosoever honours his own religion and condemns other religions, does so indeed through the devotion to his own religion, thinking, 'I will glorify my own religion.' But on the contrary, in so doing he injures his own religion more gravely. So concord is good. Let all listen, and be willing to listen to the doctrines professed by others.

(Emperor Asoka)

The strong and wise man who welcomes with consideration a suppliant, whether the followers of truth or untruth according to Law Divine, and/or out of love and humanity, he is the follower of Asha and his life is full of rectitude and righteousness.

(Yasna)

In the company of saints and holy people
Yours and mine are no more
Only Thine, O Lord.
No one an enemy, none a stranger
As friends we get on with each other.
What the Lord wills is good.
This wisdom is received in blessing from saints
The One Lord is with us all.

(Adi Granth)

Think not of the faults of others, of what they have done or not done.
Think rather of your own sins, of things you have done or not done.

(Dhammapada)

Judge not, that ye be not judged.   For with what judgement ye judge, ye
shall be judged: and with what measure ye mete, it shall be measured
unto you.   And why beholdest thou the mote that is in thy brother's eye,
but considerest not the beam that is in thine own eye?   Or how wilt thou
say to thy brother, 'Let me cast out the mote out of thine eye'; and lo,
the beam is in thine own eye?   Thou hypocrite, cast out first the beam
out of thine own eye; and then shalt thou see clearly to cast out the
mote out of thy brother's eye.

(The New Testament)

Beware lest ye offend the feelings of anyone, or sadden the heart of any
person, or move the tongue in reproach of, and finding fault with
anybody.   Beware, beware that any one rebuke or reproach a soul,
though he may be an ill-wisher or an ill-doer.

(Tablets of 'Abdu'l-Baha)

Let none deceive another,
Or despise any being in any state.
Let none through anger or ill-will
Wish harm upon another.
Even as a mother protects with her life
Her child, her only child,
So with a boundless heart
Should one cherish all living beings:
Radiating kindness over the entire world:
Spreading upwards to the skies,
And downwards to the depths:
Outwards and unbounded,
Freed from hatred and ill-will.
Whether standing or walking, seated or lying down
Free from drowsiness,
One should sustain this recollection.

(Sutta-Nipata)

O God, help us not to condemn or oppose what we do not understand.

(William Penn)

Virtues

Sing hymns at sunrise, remember God while doing chores
The Guru favours a disciple
Who remembers God with every breath.

(Adi Granth)

So, let all strive with thought, word and deed to satisfy Mazda.
Let each one choose to perform good deeds as his worship.

(Yasna)

A good character is, verily, the best mantle from God.   With it He
adorneth the temple of His loved ones.   By my life!   The light of a good
character surpasseth the light of the sun and the radiance thereof.

(The Advent of Divine Justice)

Truth is supreme
But higher than truth is truthful living.

(Adi Granth)

Truthfulness is the foundation of all human virtues.   Without truthfulness,
progress and success, in all the worlds of God, are impossible for any
soul.   When this holy attribute is established in man, all the divine
qualities will be acquired.

(Baha'i World Faiths)

Hear and give heed to these truths, O, Men and Women.
Strive to avoid the lures of this material life and stop the progress of
untruth and deceit.

(Yasna)

The man who wisely controls his senses as a good driver controls his
horses, and who is free from lower passions and pride, is admired even by
the gods.

(Sutta-Nipata)

Those who can avoid the bondage of [sinful] acts can attain liberation;
and those who have obtained liberation are free from bondage.
O Man!   Control yourself and you will be free from misery.

Renouncing anger, pride, deceit and greed one is able to free himself from
bondage of all acts.

(Acharanga Sutra)

Goodness, love, grace and gentleness,
courtesy, friendship and modesty,
honesty, penance and chastity,
charity, respect, reverence and truthfulness,
purity and self-control,
wisdom and worship -
all these together are perfect virtue,
and are the word of the loving Lord.

(Tamil Saivism)

This is what should be done
By one who is skilled in goodness,
And one who knows the path of peace:
Let them be able and upright,
Straightforward and gentle in speech,
Humble and not conceited,
Contented and easily satisfied,
Unburdened with duties and frugal in their ways,
Peaceful and calm, and wise and skilful,
Not proud and demanding in nature,
Let them not do the slightest thing
That the wise would later reprove.

(Sutta-Nipata)

The humble, meek, merciful, just, pious and devout souls are everywhere
of one religion and when death has taken off the mask, they will know
one another, though the divers liveries they wear here make them
strangers

(William Penn)

Blessed are the poor in spirit: for theirs is the kingdom of heaven
Blessed are they that mourn: for they shall be comforted.
Blessed are the meek: for they shall inherit the earth.
Blessed are they that hunger and thirst after righteousness: for they shall
be filled.
Blessed are the merciful: for they shall obtain mercy.
Blessed are the pure in heart: for they shall see God.
Blessed are the peacemakers: for they shall be called the sons of God.
Blessed are they that have been persecuted for righteousness sake: for
theirs is the kingdom of heaven.

(The New Testament)

A certain devata addressed the Buddha:
Many gods and men, wishing for well-being, have pondered over those things that constitute auspicious performances.
Tell us what is the highest auspicious performance

The Buddha:
Not to associate with fools, but to associate with the wise and to honour those who are worthy of honour; this is the most auspicious performance.

To reside in a congenial environment, to have done meritorious deeds in the past and to set oneself in the right course; this is the most auspicious performance.

A good, all-round education, [appreciation of] the Arts, a highly-trained discipline and pleasant speech; this is the most auspicious performance.

Supporting one's father and mother, cherishing wife and children and a peaceful occupation; this is the most auspicious performance.

Liberality, dutiful conduct, the helping of relatives and blameless actions; this is the most auspicious performance.

Ceasing and abstaining from evil, abstention from intoxicating drinks and diligence in virtue; this is the most auspicious performance.

Reverence, humility, contentment, gratitude and timely hearing of the Dhamma; this is the most auspicious peformance.

Forbearance, obedience, association with exemplars of the Dhamma-life and participation in religious discussions; this is the most auspicious performance.

Self-control, perception of the Noble Truths and the realization of Nibbana; this is the most auspicious performance.

If one's mind is sorrowless, stainless and secure [in Nibbana] and is not disturbed when affected by worldly vicissitudes; this is the most auspicious performance.

Those who thus acting are everywhere unconquered, attain happiness everywhere - to them these are the most auspicious performances.

(Sutta-Nipata)

Decide to be happy
render others happy
proclaim your joy
love passionately your miraculous life
do not listen to promises
do not wait for a better world
be grateful for every moment of life
switch on and keep on the positive buttons in yourself, those marked
optimism, serenity, confidence, positive thinking, love.
Pray and thank God every day
meditate - smile - laugh
whistle - sing - dance
look with fascination at everything
fill your lungs and heart with liberty
be yourself fully and immensely
act like a king or queen unto Death.
Feel God in your body, mind, heart and soul
and be convinced of eternal life and resurrection.

(Robert Muller)

O Allah! give us steadfastness in obedience and keep us far from sin.
Give us sincerity in intention, and knowledge of that which is sacred;
bestow on us guidance and constancy, seal our tongues with reason and
wisdom, fill our hearts with knowledge and learning, keep us clean from
within from what is forbidden and from those things of which we are
uncertain, keep our hands from oppression and stealing, hide from our
eyes immorality and treachery, and close our ears to foolish talk and
calumny.
Grant this through Thy Overflowing Generosity and Thy Mercy, O Merciful
and Compassionate!

(The Holy Qur'an)

INTER-FAITH SERVICES

A WORLD CONGRESS OF FAITHS SERVICE

(dating from the early nineteen fifties)

ORDER OF SERVICE

OPENING SENTENCES FROM THE BIBLES OF THE WORLD

HYMN

One holy church of God appears
Through every age and race,
Unwasted by the lapse of years,
Unchanged by changing place.

From oldest time, on furthest shores,
Beneath the pine or palm,
One unseen presence she adores,
With silence or with psalm.

Her priests are all God's faithful sons,
To serve the world raised up;
The pure in heart her baptised ones,
Love, her communion cup.

The truth is her prophetic gift,
The soul her sacred page;
And feet on mercy's errand swift
Do make her pilgrimage.

O Living Church! thine errand speed;
Fulfil thy task sublime !
With bread of life earth's hunger feed;
Redeem the evil time.

PRAYER

THE FIRST LESSON

CANTICLE   *Isaiah*

GLAD TIDINGS

The spirit of the Lord is upon me, -
Because he hath anointed me to preach the gospel to the poor;

He hath sent me to heal the broken-hearted,
To preach deliverance to the captives, and recovering of sight to the blind,

To set at liberty them that are bruised,
To preach the acceptable year of the Lord.

To give unto them that mourn a garland for ashes, -
The oil of joy for mourning, the garment of praise
for the spirit of heaviness;

That they might be called trees of righteousness, -
The planting of the Lord, that he might be glorified.

For as the earth bringeth forth her bud,
And as the garden causeth the things that are sown in it to come forth;

So the Lord God will cause righteousness and praise
To spring forth before all nations.

THE SECOND LESSON

CANTICLE   *Bhagavad Gita*

THE PATH TO HEAVENLY BIRTH

Fearlessness, singleness of soul,
The will always to strive for wisdom;
Opened hand and governed appetites;
And piety and love of lonely study;

Humbleness, uprightness, heed to injure nought which lives,
Truthfulness, slowness unto wrath,
A mind that lightly letteth go what others prize,
And equanimity and charity which spieth no man's faults;

And tenderness towards all that suffer;
A contented heart, fluttered by no desires;
A bearing mild, modest and grave.
With manhood nobly mixed,

With patience, fortitude and purity;
An unrevengeful spirit, never given to rate itself too high

Such be the signs of him whose feet are set
On that fair path which leads to heavenly birth !

THE THIRD LESSON

CANTICLE

The Buddha

BUDDHIST BEATITUDES
(to be sung softly, all seated)

Not to serve the foolish, but to serve the wise;
To honour those worthy of honour - this is the greatest blessing.

Much insight and education, self-control and pleasant speech,
And whatever word be well spoken - this is the greatest blessing.

To live righteously, to give help to kindred,
To follow a peaceful calling - this is the greatest blessing.

To be long-suffering and meek, to abhor and cease from evil,
Not to be weary in well doing - this is the greatest blessing.

To be gentle, to be patient under reproof,
To be charitable, act virtuously - this is the greatest blessing.

Reverence and humility, contentment and gratitude,
To be pure, to be temperate - this is the greatest blessing.

To dwell in a pleasant land with right desires in the heart,
To bear the remembrance of good deeds - this is the greatest blessing.

Beneath the stroke of life's changes, the mind that shaketh not,
Without grief or passion - this is the greatest blessing.

On every side are invincible they who do acts like these,
On every side they walk in safety - and theirs is the greatest blessing.

VOLUNTARY

LET US PRAY

in words of Muhammed

In the name of the merciful and compassionate God.   Praise belongs to God, the Lord
of the worlds, the merciful, the compassionate.   Thee do we serve and thee do we ask
for aid.   Guide us in the right path.

In words from the Zend Avesta

The Creator, Lord of Light, praise we.
The Teacher, Lord of Purity, praise we.
The day-times praise we.
The pure water praise we.
The stars, the moon, the sun, the trees, praise we.
The mountains, the pastures, dwellings and fountains, praise we....
The well-created animals praise we.
We praise all good men; we praise all good women.
We praise thee, our dwelling-place, O Earth.
We praise thee, O God, Lord of the dwelling place.

Amen

In words of Jesus Christ

Our Father who art in heaven, hallowed be thy name. Thy Kingdom come, Thy will be done, on earth as it is in Heaven.   Give us this day our daily bread and forgive us our trespasses, as we forgive them who trespass against us.   And lead us not into temptation.   But deliver us from evil for thine is the Kingdom, the power and the glory, for ever and ever.

Amen

HYMN

AKBAR'S DREAM

Of each fair plant the choicest blooms I scan,
For of the garden of the King I'm free
To wreathe a crown for every Mussulman,
Brahmin and Buddhist, Christian and Parsee.

Shall rose cry unto lotus, 'No flower thou' ?
Palm call to cypress, 'I alone am fair' ?
Shall mango say to melon from his bough
'Mine is the one fruit Allah did prepare' ?

Look how the living pulse of Allah beats,
Like rhythmic music through his far-flung spheres;
And light of earth with light of heaven meets
Where'er the heart of man the Good reveres.

I hate the rancour of their castes and creeds,
I let men worship as their hearts commend.
I cull from every faith the noblest deeds,
And bravest soul for counsellor and friend.

And stone by stone I'll rear a sacred fane,
A temple, neither Pagod, Mosque nor Church,
Lofty and open-door'd, where all may gain
The blessing breathed by God on souls that search.

The sun shall rise at last when creed and race
Shall bear false witness each of each no more.

7. HINDU WORSHIP AND PRAYER IN THE CONTEXT OF INTER-FAITH WORSHIP

Ranchor Prime

To understand Hindu worship it is important to be familiar with the underlying principle of Hindu prayer which can be summed up in the sequence *sravanam kirtanam vishnu smaranam*.

'Sravanam' means Hearing. Prayer begins with hearing of the sacred. When I hear a sacred sound, such as a name of God or a description of the activities of God, or of holy persons devoted to God, my attention is drawn towards God and my soul is inspired. 'Kirtanam' means Chanting. Speaking or singing about the divine is the essence of prayer. By using my tongue to sing hymns or mantras glorifying God, or to describe the path to God, my heart is focused on the divine. After hearing and chanting comes 'Smaranam', Remembering. Hearing and chanting about Vishnu leads to remembrance of Vishnu. To remember God at all times is the essence of all spiritual instructions. This principle is not just reserved for the temple or place of worship, it is for anywhere and anytime. Constant spiritual remembrance leads to a life of service to God, where every action is sanctified by the thought of the divine and the worshipper carries God in his or her heart. As Krishna says in Bhagavad Gita: 'Those who remember me without deviation obtain me easily because of their constant engagement in devotional service.' (8.14)

The hearing-chanting-remembering principle is reinforced by the addition of 'satsang', the company of holy persons. Hearing is especially effective if it is from a holy person who has love for God. Furthermore, hearing and chanting are both enhanced if they are shared in the company of other worshippers. All worshippers can be considered as lovers of God. Such group sharing or 'satsang' is the basic activity of worship in any Hindu temple.

Considering this stress on the act of hearing and chanting, most Hindus would feel a natural sense of community with all who gather to worship God, regardless of their particular faith. They would have an empathy and sensitivity to hearing the words of another's faith in God, or even, as in the case of Buddhism, another's words of insight or instruction on the spiritual path, because so much of Hindu worship is composed of just this - hearing inspirational words or sacred hymns from spiritual teachers or just from other worshippers. Hinduism has a long tradition of giving honour and hospitality to any person of faith and such honour brings grace to the one who offers it to a sincere person of the spirit.

Another feature of Hindu worship is its multiplicity.   In many ways Hinduism has always been its own multi-faith society.   The Hindu tradition recognises that God appears in many forms at many different times and teaches many paths.   Even the Bhagavad Gita, the central scripture for the majority of Hindus today, teaches at least three paths.   Variety has always been a necessary part of Hindu tradition, which recognises that each of us is an individual with particular spiritual needs.   Perhaps this is in part due to the belief in re-incarnation, because it assumes that the journey to God is longer and more demanding than can be encompassed by most of us in a single lifetime.   Further, the cosmic context of Hinduism is far-flung.   Hindu scriptures teach that there are many levels of reality and on all of them worship of God is going on.   On higher planes there are 'devas' or demigods, who have been given greater powers than us and can themselves grant boons to their worshippers.   On these higher planes are types of worship and faith that do not exist here, or at least only partially.   And beyond these higher planes is the Svargaloka, the heavenly abodes of different gods such as Brahma and Indra, all of whom have their devotees.   Within Hinduism there is also the basic division between worshippers of Shiva (Shaivites) and worshippers of Vishnu (Vaishnavas), as well as others who worship the Goddess Durga in one or other of her many manifestations.   All this means that Hindus are naturally at home in the multifaith or interfaith world.   Yet ultimately, the theistic Vaishnavas and Shaivites believe in an eternal Kingdom of God which lies beyond all other planes of existence.   A simple devotion to the supreme God of Grace, whatever name he may be known by, is therefore esteemed as the highest expression of spirituality, as described in Bhagavad Gita :   'Giving up all other paths just surrender yourself to Me.   I will release you from all your sins.   Do not fear.' (18.64)

Finally, a word must be said about Hindu deity worship, sometimes wrongly called idol worship, which it decidedly is not.   An idol is something set up in place of God (there are plenty of idols all round us today) whereas the image of the deity in a Hindu temple is made strictly according to ancient scriptural tradition to represent God in a form which the worshipper will recognise.   The temple becomes the home of the deity, a place of sanctity where devotion and service to God are focused, where the great invisible Spirit becomes visible to allow the ordinary devotee to offer prayers and service and to see the otherwise unseeable form of God.   It is a place where the visible and the invisible, the tangible and the intangible, meet.   To think that the deity is simply a statue or idol is to make a travesty of this ancient tradition.   For the most part Hindus welcome outside visitors to their temples, as one would welcome a visitor to one's own home.   All they would ask is that the visitor respect the devotions and prayers which are offered to the deity for what they are: simple acts of devotion to God on the part of ordinary people of faith.

Before one altar Truth shall Peace embrace,
And Love and Justice kneeling shall adore.

A paraphrase of Tennyson's poem by Will Hayes

SERMON

HYMN

GATHER US IN

Gather us in, thou Love that fillest all;
Gather the rival faiths within thy fold;
Throughout the nations sound the clarion call;
Beneath Love's banner all shall be enrolled !

Gather us in; we worship only thee;
In varied names we stretch a common hand;
In diverse forms a common soul we see;
In many ships we seek one spirit land.

Thine is the mystic life great India craves;
Thine is the Parsee's sin-destroying beam;
Thine is the Buddhist's rest from tossing waves;
Thine is the empire of vast China's dream.

Thine is the Roman's strength without his pride;
Thine is the Greek's glad world without its graves;
Thine is Judaea's law with love beside,
Thine is the Christian's faith - the grace that saves.

Some seek a Father in the heaven above;
Some ask a human image to adore;
Some crave a spirit, vast as life and love;
Within thy mansions, we have all and more.

Gather us in, thou love that fillest all;
Gather the rival faiths within thy fold;
Throughout the nations sound the clarion call;
Beneath Love's banner all shall be enrolled !

G. Matheson (altered)

CONCLUDING COLLECT

BENEDICTION

CIVIC SERVICE

23rd June 1991

at dashmesh Darbar Gurdwara

Order of Service

1.   Welcome
by the Mayor's Religious Adviser, Mr A.S.Bansal

2.   Reading
From the Holy Book of the Sikhs - the GRANTH SAHIB.   In accordance with Sikh tradition the Priest will open the Granth Sahib and read from whichever page it opens at.

3.   Hymn (Sung in Punjabi)

Pauri

Whatever work, thou desirest to do, tell that to
the Lord.   He shall accomplish thy affair.   The
True Guru bears true testimony to it.
By the company of the Saints, thou shalt taste
the treasure of the Name-Nectar.
The merciful Lord, the destroyer of dread,
preserves the honour of His slave.
Nanak, sing thou the praises of God and thou
shalt see the invisible Lord.

4.   Reading

From the BOOK OF RUTH.   Cllr Burns has chosen to read the story of Ruth because of its relevance to Newham's multicultural society.   Like Naomi, many people in Newham have left their homelands because of famine and other dangers.   Others like Ruth have followed in the footsteps of loved ones to settle in a strange land where their differences are noticed and commented upon.   We cannot change these differences, nor shall we try to do so.   Although Ruth says 'Thy people shall be my people and thy God my God', there is no evidence of conversion and Ruth remains a Moabitess throughout.   Yet Boaz calls on the Lord to reward Ruth for her devotion to Naomi and the goodness that is within her heart.   Thus the story of Ruth is one of acceptance of other races and religions and of respect for those who are different to ourselves.   This is a message for our times.

Cllr Jacquelin Burns.   Leader of the Conservative Group - Newham Council.

5. Hymn (Sung in Punjabi)

Ramkali 5th Guru

Some call on the Lord, 'Ram, Ram' and some 'Khuda'.
Some serve Him as 'Gosain', and some as 'Allah'
He is the Cause of causes and is Bountiful
Some talk of the Extender of mercy and some of the Merciful. (*Pause*).
Some bathe at the Hindu's pilgrim stations and some make the pilgrimage to Mecca.
Some perform Hindu worship and some bow their heads in the Muslim fashion,
Some read the Vedas and some the Muslim religious books.
Some wear blue robes and some white.
One calls himself Muslim and one calls himself Hindu.
One desires the paradise of the Muslims and one the heaven of Hindus.
Says Nanak, he who realises God's will knows the secret of the Lord Master.

6. Reading

From '*Chaos and Community*' by Martin Luther King.

Mr Jack Hart M.B.E.   Freeman of the London Borough of Newham.

7. Hymn (Sung in Pubjabi)'

Parbhati

Firstly God created light and then, by His Omnipotence, made all the mortals.
From the One light has welled up the entire universe.
Then who is good and who is bad ?
O men, my brethren, stray ye not in doubt.
Creation is in the Creator and the Creator is in Creation.   He is fully filling all places.
(*Pause*).
Clay is but the same, but the Fashioner has fashioned it in various ways.
There is no fault with the vessel of clay, nor is there any fault with the potter.
He, the One True Lord, is amidst all and it is in His will that everything is done.
Whosoever realises the Lord's will, he alone knows the One Lord and he alone is said
to be his slave.
The Lord is invisible and can be seen not.   The Guru has blessed me with sweet
molasses of His Name.
Says Kabir, my doubt has been dispelled and I now see the Immaculate Lord every
where.

8. Bidding Prayers   *Led by Cllr Alec Kellaway, Leader of Lib.Dem Group.*

Lord, we pray for our Mayor, Amarjit Singh, and we ask
that you grant him the wisdom and the strength to carry
out his duties in the coming year.   Lord hear us.

Congregation :   Lord graciously hear us.

Lord, we pray for Leela his wife and for his children, that they may love and support him in his work.   Lord hear us.

Congregation :   Lord graciously hear us.

Lord, we pray that your guidance will light the path of Newham Council, its Elected Members and its Staff, as they strive in their work for the Community.   Lord hear us.

Congregation :   Lord graciously hear us.

Lord, we ask that in your mercy and compassion you will look kindly on the whole Community of Newham.

Congregation :   Lord graciously hear us.

9.   **Hymn** (Sung in Punjabi)

Sri Rag, Fifth Guru.
I receive all joys if Him alone I obtain.   The invaluable human life becomes fruitful, if the True Name be repeated.
He, whose brow bears such a name, obtains the Lord's presence through the Guru.
O' my Soul! fix thy attention on the One Lord.
Without One (God), all else is but an entanglement.   The love of mammon is all false. (Pause).

If the True Guru casts His merciful glance, I enjoy the happinesses of lakhs of empires.
Were he to bless me with His Name even for a trice, my soul and body will become cool
They, who are so pre-ordained hold fast the feet of the True Guru.
Fruitful is the moment and fruitful the time when love for the True Lord is embraced.
Suffering and sorrow do not touch him, who has the support of God's Name.
Whom the Guru takes out, seizing by the arm he crosses the (Sea of Life).
Embellished and immaculate is the place where the Saint's congregation is held.
He alone, who has found the Perfect Guru, obtains the place of protection.
Nanak has founded his house on that (ground) where there is no death, birth and old age.

10.   **Reading**

From Psalm 103
'Bless the Lord, O my soul and all that is within me'.

Councillor Stephen Timms.   Leader of the Council.

11.   **Conclusion**

By the Mayor's Religious Adviser,
Mr A.S. Bansal

DUDLEY COUNCIL OF FAITHS

ONE WORLD WEEK 1992

PRAYER FOR WORLD PEACE

Thursday 22nd October

The Dudley Day Centre, Stafford Street

Prayers will be offered by members of the Muslim, Sikh, Buddhist, Hindu and Christian communities in Dudley.   Silence will be kept after each offering of prayer.

Offerings placed in the Glass Jar will be given to the work of the International Red Cross and Red Crescent Movement.

The emblem of the red cross was instituted by the Geneva Convention of 1864 to ensure the protection of those wounded in war and those who care for them.   A red crescent emblem made its appearance a few years later.   The cross had been adopted as a tribute to Switzerland, and had not been intended to have any religious significance.   In 1876, however, during the Russo-Turkish war, the Ottoman Society for Relief to the Wounded replaced it by a red crescent.   This emblem has since been adopted by a number of countries in the Islamic world.   It is recognized as having equal status with the red cross, and as such is mentioned in the 1949 Geneva Conventions and their Additional Protocols.

'By its humanitarian work and the dissemination of its ideals, the Movement promotes a lasting peace, which is not simply the absence of war, but is a dynamic process of co-operation among all States and people, co-operation founded on respect for freedom, independence, national sovereignty, equality, human rights, as well as on a fair and equitable distribution of resources to meet the needs of peoples.'   (from guidelines adopted in 1984)

A Muslim Prayer

22   ALLAH is He, than Whom
There is no other God;
Who knows (all things)
Both secret and open
He Most Gracious,
Most Merciful

23   ALLAH is He, than Whom
There is no other God;
The Sovereign, The Holy One,
The Source of PEACE
     (and Perfection),
The Guardian of Faith,
The Exalted in Might
The Irresistible, The Supreme

Glory to ALLAH! (High is He)
Above the partners
They attribute to Him.

24   He is ALLAH, The Creator
The Evolver,
The Bestower of Forms (or colours)
To Him belong
The Most Beautiful Names;
Whatever is in
The heavens and on earth,
Doth declare
His Praises and Glory;
And He is the Exalted
In Might, The Wise
    (Sura Hashar from the Holy Qur'an:
    p.1528 and 1529 in the version by
    Abdullah Yusuf Ali)

A Sikh Prayer

In the beginning God brought forth His Light.
From His Creative Power came all beings.

From the One Light the entire universe came forth.
So who is good and who is bad ?

Stray not in doubt, O Siblings of Destiny !

The Creator is in the Creation,
   The Creation is in the Creator,
He is ever-present, pervading everywhere.

The clay is the same, while it is fashioned
   into many forms by the Master Potter.

There is no fault with the vessel of clay,
   as there is no fault with the Potter.

Within all is the One True Lord.
It is by His Will that all exist.

One who realizes God's Will, comes to know God.
He is the true servant of the Lord.

The invisible Lord cannot be seen.
The Guru has blessed me with this sweet realization.

Says Kabir: My doubt is dispelled.
   I see the Perfect Pure Lord everywhere.

(Aval Allah)

A Buddhist Litany of Peace

As we are together, praying for Peace, let us be truly with each other.
SILENCE

Let us be at peace within ourselves, our bodies and our minds, our emotions and our spirit.
SILENCE

Let us return to ourselves and become wholly ourselves.
SILENCE

Let us be aware of the source of being common to us all and to all living things.
SILENCE

Evoking the presence of the Great Compassion, let us open our hearts to receive compassion -
for ourselves and for all living beings.
SILENCE

Let us pray that all living beings may realise that they are all brothers and sisters, all nourished from the same source of life.

SILENCE

Let us pray that we ourselves may cease to be the cause of suffering to each other.

SILENCE

Let us pledge ourselves to live in a way which will not deprive other beings of air, water, food, shelter, or the chance to live.

SILENCE

With humility, with awareness of the uniqueness of life, and with compassion for the suffering around us, let us pray for the establishment of peace in our hearts and peace on earth.

A Hindu Prayer

O God, the Giver of Life, Remover of pains and sorrows, bestower of happiness, and creator of the universe, Thou art most luminous, pure and adorable. We meditate on Thee. May thou inspire and guide our intellect in the right direction.

(The Gayatri or Guru Mantra)

There is peace in the heavenly region, there is peace in the atmosphere; peace reigns on the earth; there is coolness in the water; the medicinal herbs are healing; the plants are peace-giving; there is harmony in the celestial objects and perfection in eternal knowledge; everything in the universe is peaceful; peace pervades everywhere. May that peace come to me !

May there be peace, peace, peace

(Shanti Path - Hymn of Peace)

O Supreme Spirit! Lead us from untruth to truth. Lead us from darkness to light. Lead us from death to immortality.

O Lord! in Thee may all be happy. May all be free from misery, may all realise goodness, and may no one suffer pain.

A Christian Prayer

Let us in silence bring ourselves to that place of stillness,
that place of peace and wholeness.
Let us make this peace our desire for all the world.

SILENCE

People of Ireland, torn and tired of being torn ....   PEACE BE WITH YOU

SILENCE

People of Africa, exploited and tired of being exploited ....   PEACE BE WITH YOU

SILENCE

People of the Middle East, turbulent and tired of being turbulent ....   PEACE BE WITH YOU

SILENCE

People of South America, silenced and tired of being silenced ....   PEACE BE WITH YOU

SILENCE

People of India, divided and tired of being divided ....   PEACE BE WITH YOU

SILENCE

People of Russia, suspected and tired of being suspected ....   PEACE BE WITH YOU

SILENCE

(other prayers may be included in the same manner)

People of the West, privileged and tired of being privileged ....   PEACE BE WITH YOU

SILENCE

People on our hearts ....   PEACE BE WITH YOU

SILENCE

May the God of all people and Jesus Christ give us grace and peace this day and every day. Amen.

A Prayer for All to Share

The International Prayer for Peace

Lead me from death to life, from falsehood to truth.
Lead me from despair to hope, from fear to trust.
Lead me from hate to love, from war to peace.
Let peace fill our heart, our world, our universe.

(The words, adapted from the Upanishads, were used by Mother Teresa in 1981.
She urged everyone of all faiths to use the peace prayer daily at noon.)

World Congress of Faiths Conference 1993

At Ammerdown, Nr. Radstock, Bath

20 November 1993

The service is in four parts

1. Thanksgiving

2. Penitence for
   prejudice between religions

   indifference to suffering

   abuse of nature

3. The strength our Faiths offer

4. Our hope

Leader   During this year many people have learned to rejoice at the variety of religions and the enrichment that others bring to our own lives.

Litany

Reader I   Thank you and praise you for our Muslim brothers and sisters, for their commitment in prayer and faithfulness in worship.

Thank you and praise you for our Sikh sisters and brothers, for their warm hospitality and public witness to their faith.

Thank you and praise you for our Baha'i brothers and sisters, for their genuine openness and overriding desire for unity.

Thank you and praise you for our Buddhist sisters and brothers, for their peace and relinquishing of self.

Thank you and praise you for our Christian brothers and sisters, for their message of love and their practice of forgiveness.

Thank you and praise you for our Jewish sisters and brothers, for their enriching symbols of worship and their cherishing of tradition.

Thank you and praise you for our Hindu brothers and sisters, for their open-hearted acceptance of others and kindly disposition towards those of other faiths.

Thank you and praise you for our Jain sisters and brothers, for their deep respect for life and practice of nonviolence.

Thank you and praise you for our brothers and sisters of indigenous traditions, for their reverence of nature and their ancient and still living cultures.

ALL   Thank you and praise you for those of every faith tradition, named and unnamed, for the variety and richness of their spiritualities, for our common quest for truth, our yearning after love, our longing for peace and commitment to justice. Ever unite us we pray, help us and inspire us, that we might live more truly for you throughout our lives.
Amen.

© *From the Week of Prayer for World Peace*

SILENCE

Leader   There is still, sadly, much prejudice and misuse of religion.

Reader 2
     Lord of all,
     we stand in awe before you,
     impelled by the visions of the harmony of all people,
     We are children of many traditions -
     inheritors of shared wisdom and tragic misunderstandings,
     of proud hopes and humble successes,
     Now it is time for us to meet
     in memory and truth
     in courage and trust.
     in love and promise.

Forms of prayer for Jewish Worship

SILENCE

Leader   There is indifference to the sufferings of others.

Reader 3

Poverty is
- a knee-level view from your bit of pavement;
- a battered, upturned cooking pot and countable ribs;
- coughing from your steel-banded lungs, alone, with your face to the wall;
- shrunken breasts and a three-year-old who cannot stand;
- the ringed fingers, the eyes averted, and a five-paise piece in your hand;
- smoking the babus' cigarette butts to quieten the fiend in your belly;
- a husband without a job, without a square meal a day, without energy, without hope;
- being at the mercy of everyone further up the ladder because you are a threat to their self-respect;
- a hut of tins and rags and plastic bags, in a warren of huts you cannot stand up in, where your neighbours live at one arm's length across the lane;
- a man who cries out in silence;
- nobody listening, for everyone's talking;
- the prayer withheld;
- the heart withheld;
- the hand withheld; yours and mine.

ALL   Lord, teach us to hate our poverty of spirit.

Litany from Calcutta.

SILENCE

Leader   There is misuse of this beautiful earth.

The Spirit who brought beauty to the Earth is not pleased.   The Earth grows ugly with misuse.   Are you listening ?

The Spirit who brought forth all creatures is being destroyed.   Are you listening ?

The Spirit who gave humans life and a path to walk together is not pleased.   You are losing your humanity and your footsteps stray from the path.   Are you listening ?

O God, who created the Earth in goodness and in beauty, Forgive all that we have done to harm the Earth.
O God, you have filled the Earth with food for our sustenance, Forgive us for not sharing the gifts of the Earth.
You have created us, O God, of one blood throughout the Earth,
Forgive us for not living as sisters and brothers should.

> O Great Spirit of God
> Whose breath gives life to the world
> and whose voice is heard in the soft breeze
> we need your strength and wisdom.
> May we walk in Beauty
> May our eyes ever behold the red and purple sunset.
> Make us wise so that we may understand what you have taught us.
> Help us learn lessons you have hidden in every leaf and rock.

Based on Native American prayers

SILENCE

HYMN

Human Rights

For the healing of the nations,
      Lord, we pray with one accord;
for a just and equal sharing
      of the things that earth affords
To a life of love in action
      help us rise and pledge our word.

Lead us, Father, into freedom,
      from despair your world release;
that, redeemed from war and hatred,
      all may come and go in peace.
Show us how through care and goodness
      fear will die and hope increase.

All that kills abundant living,
      let it from the earth be banned;
pride of status, race or schooling,
      dogmas that obscure your plan.
In our common quest for justice
      may we hallow life's brief span.

Fred Kaan

© 1968 Stainer and Bell Ltd, London, England.

Leader   Our search is not just for better relations between religious people but for a new more peaceful and more just world.

In our work, we need the strength that our religious traditions offer.

No one can put together what has crumbled into dust, but you can restore a conscience turned to ashes; you can restore to its former beauty a soul lost without hope. With you, there is nothing that cannot be redeemed; you are love, you are creator and redeemer; we praise you, singing Alleluia.

Father Gregory Petrou. Composed just prior to his death in prison under Stalin.

Whoever goes to the Lord for safety, whoever remains under the protection of the Almighty, can say to Him 'You are my Defender and Protector. You are my God, in you I trust'. He will keep you safe from all hidden dangers.

Psalm 91.1,2 & 3

The servants of God are those who show patience, firmness and self-control, who are true in word and deed, who worship devoutly, who spend time in the way of God; and so pray for forgiveness in the early hours of the morning.

Qur'an 3.15 & 17

SILENCE

Leader   In helping others our hope is renewed.

JOURNEY ON IN HOPE

Dear world, being disabled does not mean necessarily not being able to lead a normal life, within limitations. It is important to look at disability, not as the best that ever happened to you, but not the worst either. It has been 18 years since I had my car accident, which made me disabled. The wheelchair didn't prevent me from studying and becoming a lawyer, to work for disabled people. My social work with the poor and needy took me to represent the people of my own town when I became an alderman, and today I represent my state Sao Paulo, with a population of 36 million people, in Congress. At 37, I am the proud mother of Diego, 2, and Rodrigo, 5, and I had both of them from natural labour. Life taught me something very important ! Happiness does not mean a pair of legs, or eyes, or ears, but the will to take part and share with others, respecting them as human beings and being respected as such.

Celia Leae, Brazil.

SILENCE

Leader   Prayer

God of mystery, you are far beyond our telling and the tales of our imagining, far beyond the doctrines and the dogmas of our believing. When we try and trap you inside, you are outside. When we claim you as our own, you are another's. When in fear we shut you out, you are found within. When in anger we blame and accuse and judge our neighbour, we only condemn ourselves and blaspheme your name. Your love embraces all and loses no one. Your care extends to every person and all things. In such love is our cherishing and our peace, and in such love may we journey on in hope.

Week of Prayer for World Peace

Finally   # WE SHALL OVERCOME

All shall hold hands as we sing this.

We shall overcome,
We shall overcome,
We shall overcome some day,
Oh, deep in my heart I do believe
We shall overcome some day.

We'll walk hand in hand,
We'll walk hand in hand,
We'll walk hand in hand some day,
Oh, deep in my heart I do believe
We shall overcome some day.

The truth will make us free,
The truth will make us free,
The truth will make us free some day,
Oh, deep in my heart I do believe
We shall overcome some day.

The Lord will see us through,
The Lord will see us through,
The Lord will see us through some day,
Oh, deep in my heart, I do believe
We shall overcome some day.

We shall overcome,
We shall overcome,
We shall overcome some day,
Oh, deep in my heart, I do believe
We shall overcome some day.

We shall live in peace,
We shall live in peace,
We shall live in peace some day,
Oh, deep in my heart I do believe
We shall overcome some day.

We are not afraid,
We are not afraid,
We are not afraid today;
Oh deep in my heart I do believe
We shall overcome some day.

The whole wide world around,
The whole wide world around,
The whole wide world around some day,
Oh, deep in my heart I do believe
We shall overcome some day.

Zilphia Horton, Frank Hamilton, Guy Carawan, Pete Seeger
© 1960, 1963 Ludlow Music Inc., New York, U.S.A.
Assigned to TRO ESSEX MUSIC LTD., London SW10 0SZ

WESTMINSTER ABBEY

AN OBSERVANCE
for
COMMONWEALTH DAY

In the presence of

HER MAJESTY THE QUEEN

HEAD OF THE COMMONWEALTH

and

HIS ROYAL HIGHNESS THE DUKE OF EDINBURGH

Monday 10 March 1997, 3.15 p.m.

AT 3.15 P.M. THE PROCESSION moves through the centre aisle of the Nave and through the South Quire Aisle into the Quire. Flags of the Commonwealth Countries, led by the Commonwealth Flag, are carried in procession.
When all are in their places the National Anthem is sung by all present:

GOD SAVE THE QUEEN

God save our gracious Queen,
Long live our noble Queen,
    God save the Queen.
Send her victorious,
Happy and glorious,
Long to reign over us;
    God save the Queen.

Not on this land alone,
But be God's mercies known
From shore to shore.
Lord, make the nations see
That we in unity
Should form one family
The wide world o'er.

Music: from *Thesaurus Musicus* (c1743), arranged by Gordon Jacob (1895-1984)

All sit for **The Commonwealth Day Message 1997** from Her Majesty The Queen, Head of the Commonwealth.

all stand to sing **The Hymn**

Praise, my soul, the King of heaven
    To his feet thy tribute bring;
ransomed, healed, restored, forgiven,
    who like me his praise should sing
      Alleluia, Alleluia,
    Praise the everlasting King.
Praise him for his grace and favour
    to our fathers in distress;
Praise him still the same as ever,
    Slow to chide, and swift to bless:

Alleluia, Alleluia,
Glorious in his faithfulness.

Father-like, he tends and spares us.
Well our feeble frame he knows;
in his hands he gently bears us,
rescues us from all our foes;
Alleluia, Alleluia
widely as his mercy flows.

Angels help us to adore him
ye behold him face to face
sun and moon bow down before him
dwellers all in time and space;
Alleluia, Alleluia,
Praise with us the God of grace

Music : Praise My Soul, John Goss (1800-80)
Words : H.F. Lyte (1793-1847) based on Psalm 103

1: STEWARDSHIP OF THE EARTH

All sit for **The Reading**
chanted in Arabic, from the Qur'an, Surah 56, 63-74.   A translation reads:

Have you considered the soil you till?   Is it you who bring the crop or are We the real agent of growth?   Were it Our will We had turned it into chaff and that would have meant for you a sorry jest, as you say: 'The loss is heavy on us, we are disconsolate.'

Have you considered the water you drink?   Was it you who made it fall from the rain-clouds, or are We the rain-maker?   Had We so willed, bitter water had We sent.   How is it that you have no gratitude?

Have you considered the fire you kindle?   Was it you who made the tree to grow or are We the source of its being?   We devised it for a point of recollection and to provide solace for those who pass through desert ways.

Praise, then, each of you the Name of your great Lord.

All stand to say together the first Affirmation led by The Dean with the words:

Let us say together the first Affirmation:

We affirm our respect for the whole of the natural world and acknowledge our responsibility for exercising our stewardship with care and consideration for all its elements.

2: HUMAN WORTH

All sit for **The Reading** *from the Misnah Sanhedrin 4.5*

It is for this reason that, according to the biblical account, only one human being was created in the beginning: to teach us that anyone who destroys a single soul is considered by

Scripture as if they had destroyed the whole world, and anyone who saves a single soul as if they had saved the whole world. Also for the sake of peace among human beings, so that no one may have a right to say to another, 'My ancestor was greater than your ancestor!' And again, to proclaim the greatness of God: for we stamp many coins with one seal, and they are all alike, but the Sovereign above all sovereigns, the Holy One, who is ever to be blessed, has stamped all human beings with the seal of Adam, yet not two of them are alike. Therefore every individual must say, 'The world was created for my sake!'

All stand to say together the second Affirmation led by The Dean with the words :

Let us say together the second Affirmation:

We affirm our common faith in the dignity and unique worth of the human person irrespective of colour, class or creed.

All sit for **the anthem**, *sung by the Boys of the Westminster Abbey Choir:*

Love one another with a pure heart fervently, see that ye love one another.

Music: Samuel Sebastian Wesley (1810-76)
Words: *1 Peter* 1:22

3. JUSTICE AND PEACE

All remain seated for **The Reading** *from the Guru Granth Sahib.*

This wonder of the Lord have I beheld, my cherished beloved!
That whatever He does is righteous and just.
The Lord has made this world His play-house, my cherished beloved!
In which the players but come and go.
It is He who created this world that destined us to be born and die.
Some by uniting them to the holy Preceptor, to Himself He calls:
Some in illusion stray about.
Lord! to Thee alone is Thy extent known,
And in all Creation art Thou pervasive.
Nanak speaketh the truth, listen O saints,
That whatever the Lord does is righteous and just.

All remain seated for **The Baha'i Reading** *from The Hidden words of Baha'ullah.*

O Son of Spirit!
The best beloved of all things in My sight is Justice: turn not away therefrom if thou desirest Me, and neglect if not that I may confide in thee. By its aid thou shalt see with thine own eyes and not through the eyes of others, and shalt know of thine own knowledge and not through the knowledge of thy neighbour. Ponder this in thy heart; how it behoveth thee to be. Verily justice is My gift to thee and the sign of My loving-kindness. Set it then before thine eyes.

All stand to say together the third Affirmation led by The Dean with the words:

Let us say together the third Affirmation :

We affirm our common faith in the need to establish justice for every individual, and through common effort to secure peace and reconciliation between nations.

4. LOVE IN RELATIONSHIPS

All sit for a reading from the Sutta-Nipata words from The Discourse on Loving-Kindness.

May all beings be happy and secure, may their hearts be wholesome!

Whatever living beings there be - those mentally feeble or strong, physically long, stout or medium, short, small or large, those seen or unseen; dwelling far or near - may all beings, without exception, be happy-minded!

Let none deceive another nor despise any person whatsoever in any place; in anger or ill-will let one not wish any harm to another.

Just as a mother would protect her only child at the risk of her own life, even so, let one cultivate a boundless heart towards all beings.

Let thoughts of infinite love pervade the whole world - above, below and around - without any obstruction, without any hatred, without any enmity.

Whether standing, walking, sitting or lying down, as long as one is awake, this mindfulness should be developed; this, the wise say, is the highest conduct here.

All stand to say together the fourth Affirmation led by The Dean with the words:

Let us say together the fourth Affirmation:

We affirm our common faith in the need to assert the supremacy of love in all human relationships.

All sit

The Visual Ministry Choir sings:

> People, listen there is something that you need to know;
> too long we've been fighting, racial wars that started long ago.
> Dear Lord, for us to grow we must let go of what's been keeping us apart
> Now's the time to put the past behind.
> together all mankind can make a brand new start
> > *Refrain:*   Love has no colour; you're my brother.
> >   Love shows no evil, to no people

We know there's a difference in the colours of our skin;
so be proud of your heritage and learn from the lesson they give.
Dear Lord, for us to grow we must let go of what's been keeping us apart.
Now's the time to put the past behind,
together all mankind can make a brand new start.
Refrain: Love has no colour ...

If we can learn to love with our hearts and not our eyes -
love for all brothers,all kinds and all colours -
What a world this would be - for you and me.
Refrain: Love has no colour ...

Music: Ronald Winans (C) 1987 Zomba Enterprises Corporated
Words: Marvin Winans, Percy Bady and Ronald Winans

5. SERVICE AND SACRIFICE

All remain seated for **The Reading** from the Universal Prayers, verses 311 and 312

May all be happy.   May all be free from disease.   May all realise what is good.   May none be subject to misery.

May the wicked become virtuous.   May the virtuous attain tranquillity.   May the tranquil be free from all bonds.   May the freed make others free.

Shanti. [*Peace*] Shanti. Shanti.

All stand to say together the fifth Affirmation led by The Dean with the words:

Let us say together the fifth Affirmation:

We affirm our membership of the one human family and our concern to express it in service and sacrifice for the common good.

All sit for **The Reading** from the Gospel according to St Luke 6: 37-38 & 41-45.

Jesus said, 'Do not judge, and you will not be judged; do not condemn, and you will not be condemned; pardon, and you will be pardoned; give, and gifts will be given to you.   Good measure, pressed and shaken down and running over, will be poured into your lap;   for whatever measure you deal out to others will be dealt to you in turn.

Why do you look at the speck in your brother's eye, with never a thought for the plank in your own?   How can you say to your brother. "Brother, let me take the speck out of your eye,' when you are blind to the plank in your own?"   You hypocrite!   First take the plank out of your own eye, and then you will see clearly to take the speck out of your brother's.

There is no such thing as a good tree producing bad fruit, nor yet a bad tree producing good fruit.   Each tree is known by its own fruit;   you do not gather figs from brambles or pick grapes from thistles.   Good people produce good from the store of good within themselves; and evil people produce evil from the evil within them.   For the words that the mouth utters come from the overflowing of the heart.'

6. THE MEDITATION

All remain seated for **The Introduction**

We have heard from the teachings of the world's great religions this afternoon.   We have recognised that we are stewards - not owners - of the earth.   We have affirmed the worth of each human being, and the values by which we must strive to live.

We all fall short of these great teachings.   Men and women can, and do, live without values, but, without them, we cannot begin to live well.

Let us pray that the great ideals that we have affirmed this afternoon will increasingly be realised in the lives of individuals, and of nations, both within the Commonwealth and throughout the world.

All remain seated.

Sheona White, tenor horn, plays: Greensleeves
Music: Anonymous tune, arranged by Stuart Pullin

during which members of the London Studio Centre perform an interpretative dance.

All remain seated for a short period of silent reflection, followed by The Prayer for Peace

The Prayer for Peace

Lead me from death to life,
from falsehood to truth

Lead me from despair to hope,
from fear to trust.

Lead me from hate to love,
from war to peace.

Let peace fill our heart,
our world, our universe .....

Peace * Peace * Peace

Words:Satish Kumar, a member of the Jain community;
Prayer for Peace movement, 1981

All stand to sing **The Hymn**

When I needed a neighbour were you there, were you there?
When I needed a neighbour were you there?
And the creed and the colour and the name won't matter,
were you there?

I was hungry and thirsty, were you there, were you there?
I was hungry and thirsty, were you there?
Chorus: **And the creed ...**

I was cold, I was naked, were you there, were you there?
   I was cold, I was naked, were you there?
Chorus: **And the creed ...**

When I needed a shelter were you there, were you there?
   When I needed a shelter were you there?
Chorus: **And the creed ...**

When I needed a healer were you there, were you there?
   When I needed a healer were you there?
Chorus: **And the creed ...**

Wherever you travel I'll be there, I'll be there.
   Wherever you travel I'll be there.
Chorus: **And the creed ...**

Music: NEIGHBOUR, Sydney Carter (b 1915)
Words: Sydney Carter
© 1968 and 1973 Stainer and Bell Ltd, London, England.

All remain standing for **The Prayers**

In confidence and trust we make our prayers to God.

O God our Father, we thank you for the world you have made.   Grant that we may treasure it as the work of a loving creator, and that we may be faithful stewards of it for the sake of generations to come.
               Lord, hear us:
All   **Lord, graciously hear us.**

Jesus Christ showed your love through his life and death, and told his friends that he had come not to be served but to serve.   Grant that we too may be caring and ready to give of ourselves in all our dealings with one another.
               Lord, hear us:
All   **Lord, graciously hear us.**

Send to us your Holy Spirit, to lead us all in unity and truth, and to guide us in all our thoughts, words and actions.
               Lord, hear us
All   **Lord, graciously hear us.**

Bless the Queen, and all the nations of the Commonwealth.   Give wisdom to those who are in positions of national and international responsibility and authority; and grant to all your people justice and peace, so that men, women and children of every community may both give and receive understanding and mutual respect.
               Lord hear us:
All   **Lord, graciously hear us.**

Hear us as we pray for those who suffer through oppression, violence and war, or by means of any environmental disaster; for all those who are imprisoned, whether justly or unjustly; for the homeless and refugees; for all who are in any kind of danger; and for all those who work in any way to relieve their need and suffering.
               Lord hear us:
All   **Lord, graciously hear us.**

Eternal Light, shine into our hearts;
eternal Goodness, deliver us from evil;
eternal Power, be our support;
eternal Wisdom, scatter the darkness of our ignorance;
eternal Pity, have mercy upon us;
that with all our heart and mind and soul and strength we may seek you and be brought by
your infinite mercy to your holy presence, who are God for ever and ever.   **Amen.**

All remain standing to sing **The Hymn**

Give me joy in my heart: keep me praising;
give me joy in my heart, I pray;
Give me joy in my heart: keep me praising;
keep me praising 'til the break of day.
Sing hosanna, sing hosanna,
sing hosanna to the King of kings;
sing hosanna, sing hosanna,
sing hosanna to the King.

Give me peace in my heart: keep me resting;
give me peace in my heart, I pray;
Give me peace in my heart: keep me resting;
keep me resting 'til the break of day.
Refrain: Sing hosanna ...

Give me love in my heart: keep me serving;
Give me love in my heart, I pray;
Give me love in my heart: keep me serving;
keep me serving 'til the break of day.
Refrain: Sing hosanna ...

Music and Words: GIVE ME JOY, traditional;
arranged by Christian Strover (c) Jubilate Hymns

All remain standing for The Dean of Westminster to give

THE BLESSING

Unto God's gracious mercy and protection we commit you.   The Lord bless
and keep you.   The Lord make his face to shine upon you, and be gracious to
you.   The Lord lift his countenance upon you, and give you his peace.   **Amen.**

Words: the Aaronic blessing.   Numbers 6: 24-6

*All remain standing.   The Procession moves from the Lantern and Quire through the North
Quire aisle and the centre of the Nave to the West Door.*

The Melodians Steel Orchestra plays and the Bells of the Abbey Church are rung.

(Reproduced with the kind permission of the Council of the Joint Commonwealth Societies)

AN INTERFAITH SERVICE OF CELEBRATION

IN HONOR OF THE FIFTIETH ANNIVERSARY

OF THE FOUNDING OF THE UNITED NATIONS

SUNDAY, June 25TH, 1995   GRACE CATHEDRAL
2.00 PM   SAN FRANCISCO

Welcome to Grace Cathedral on this glorious and historic occasion.   This Interfaith Service has
been designed to give expression to the highest aspirations of the human community for
justice, freedom and peace.   Please participate fully, joining especially in the reading, the
hymn and the concluding Greeting of Peace.

PRELUDE MUSIC SUNG BY:

Sine Nomine (*The Bay Area Choir of the Church of Jesus Christ of Latter Day Saints*)

Visions in Sound (*Brahma Kumaris World Spiritual Organization*)

The Baha'i World Choir of Northern California

Muezzin Imam Rasheed Shabazz (*A Muslim Soloist*)

The Tongan Traditional Interfaith Choir

Elena Bokharova (*A Russian Soloist*)

The Interfaith Choir of San Francisco

The Sikh Dharma Choir

Cantor Roslyn Barak and the Temple Emanu-el Choir

*During the Prelude Music dignitaries will be seated.   Immediately before the Procession a
representative of the Native American Peoples will offer an invocation and chant.*

THE PROCESSION (*Please stand*)

As the Procession enters, members of the Royal Philharmonic Orchestra will play.

FANFARE FOR THE COMMON MAN
                                                                Aaron Copland

GREETING
                                          The Right Reverend William E Swing
                                                          Bishop of California

OPENING READING
                                          Read together by everyone, standing.

THE PREAMBLE TO THE UNITED NATIONS CHARTER

We the peoples of the United Nations, determined to save succeeding generations from the scourge of war, which twice in our lifetime has brought untold sorrow to mankind, and to reaffirm faith in fundamental human rights, in the dignity and worth of the human person, in the equal rights of men and women and of nations large and small, and to establish conditions under which justice and respect for the obligations arising from treaties and other sources of international law can be maintained, and to promote social progress and better standards of life in larger freedom and for these ends to practice tolerance and live together in peace with one another as good neighbors and to unite our strength to maintain international peace and security and to ensure by the acceptance of principles and the institution of methods, that armed force shall not be used, save in the common interest and to employ international machinery for the promotion of the economic and social advancement of all peoples, have resolved to combine our efforts to accomplish these aims.   Accordingly, our respective governments, through representatives assembled in the city of San Francisco, who have exhibited their full powers found to be in good and due form, have agreed to the present Charter of the United Nations and do hereby establish an international organization to be known as the United Nations.

A MOMENT OF SILENCE (*Remain standing*)

In remembrance of all those who have died while involved in humanitarian and peace missions.

MUSIC (*Please be seated*)

Sung by the Grace Cathedral Choir of Men and Boys with members of the Royal Philharmonic Orchestra

HYMN FOR A NEW AGE

Lee Hoiby

*Through the long night we have come
The sun is bright, the wars are done.
We will unite.   We will be one. A new light has begun.
Smile, heaven on our loving land,
shine blessings on our fair kingdom.
Enrich our time to come with growing love,
with joy abundant and long, prosperous days.
Man's brotherhood is born again.
The face of freedom is revealed in sunlight.
Now sing in praise of life;
with poems praise, with voices praise
with drums, with trumpets praise
God's loving Kingdom come to us,
the gift of life and the gift of freedom.
Now shall peace reign, truth be revealed, and all wounds be healed.
So was it ever meant to be,
resplendent hope of humankind
to follow the dove, the way of peace, the way of love.
So shall it be, so shall it ever be.*

©

GREETING

Dr. Boutros Boutros-Ghali
Secretary-General of the United Nations

THE MINGLING OF SACRED WATERS AND FLOWERS

The congregation is seated. Children's choirs from the Golden Gate International Children's Choir Festival will carry in procession waters and flowers from sacred sites around the world. They will be mingled in a bowl before the altar as the children sing.

THE BLUE-GREEN HILLS OF EARTH (*from Missa Gaia*)   Kim Oler, arr. Nick Page.

For the earth forever turning, for the skies, for every sea;
for our lives, for all we cherish, sing we our joyful song of peace.

For the mountains, hills and pastures in their silent majesty;
for the stars, for all the heavens, sing we our joyful song of peace.

For the sun, for rain and thunder, for the seasons' harmony;
for our lives, for all creation, sing we our joyful praise to Thee.

For the world we raise our voices, for the home that gives us birth;
in our joy we sing returning home to our blue-green hills of earth

©   Words by Kim Oler

READING

From The Parliament of World Religions' Declaration Towards a Global Ethic

MUSIC

A BAHA'I PRAYER FOR UNITY (*Please Stand*)   'Abdu'l-Baha

Sung in Persian to traditional chant by Zoreh Samadani.

O my God! O my God! Verily, I invoke thee and supplicate before thy threshold, asking thee that all thy mercies may descend upon these souls. Specialize them for thy favor and thy truth

O Lord! Unite and bind together the hearts, join in accord all the souls, and exhilarate the spirits through the signs of thy sanctity and oneness. O Lord! Make these faces radiant through the light of thy oneness. Strengthen the loins of thy servants in the service of thy kingdom.

O Lord, thou possessor of infinite mercy! O Lord of forgiveness and pardon! Forgive our sins, pardon our shortcomings, and cause us to turn to the kingdom of thy clemency, invoking the kingdom of might and power, humble at thy shrine and submissive before the glory of thine evidences.

O Lord God! Make us as waves of the sea, as flowers of the garden, united, agreed through the bounties of thy love. O Lord! Dilate the breasts through the signs of thy oneness, and make all mankind as stars shining from the same height of glory, as perfect fruits growing upon thy tree of life.

Verily, thou art the Almighty, the Self-Subsistent, the Giver, the Forgiving, the Pardoner, the Omniscient, the One Creator.

GREETING

A participant from the Interfaith Youth Conference 'Rediscovering Justice' will deliver a challenge to the gathered leaders of world religions on behalf of the young people attending the conference.

HYMN   Sung by all, standing.

ODE TO FREEDOM   Ludwig van Beethoven.

We with arms embracing millions
Kiss this earthly paradise.
Bless the stars in all their billions!
Bless the rhythm of our lives.
Friendship is our greatest treasure,
Joyfully its strains prolong.
Born of stars in pain and pleasure,
Friendship is the cosmic song.

Joined in courage, joined in passion
In our friendship we grow strong.
Reach the broken with compassion,
Teach the truth against all wrong.
Swear it, as the stars all quiver
In the deep and dazzling skies.
Swear it, as the stars' Lawgiver
Leads the chorus of our lives.

©   Original German words by Schiller
English translation by Richard Boeke

UNITY CIRCLE AND GREETING OF PEACE

Remain standing as religious leaders gather at the altar.   As they greet each other, please greet your neighbours with a sign of peace.

RECESSIONAL

FINALE FROM SYMPHONIE I   Conrad Sousa

Please remain in your seats until the procession of religious leaders and the United Nations Ambassadors have left.   Everyone is warmly invited to a simple reception in the courtyard and Huntington Park, where some of the visiting interfaith choirs will sing.

A short while into the reception the cathedral carillon will play.   Please join in a toast 'To the Human Family'.

The Opening Ceremony of Our British Interfaith Ecological Centre

Claire Dalley

This 'imaginary' service was written by Claire Dalley as part of her work as a student of Theology and World Religions at Westminster College, Oxford. Copyright for this chapter is with Westminster College.

Introduction

When we look at the use of flowers in history and the present day, their influence is almost universal. They touch many faiths and cultural systems. They are present in the symbolism, liturgy, poetry, thought and psyche of many of the world's religions. They seem to express in visual form, profound statements from the giver to the receiver.

In religions, flowers have been used to express an abundance of theology, philosophy and thought. A common theme is that of impermanence. Philosophers and poets alike have compared the short life of a bloom to the relatively short life span of a human being. For many, flowers have become a natural tool to reveal our thoughts on death and the afterlife: although the bloom dies, and retires for Autumn, Spring occurs bringing the plant back to life. This phenomenon has been used to explain beliefs about Rebirth, New Life and Resurrection.

In today's 'Post-modern' world, flowers have taken on additional meanings. They are often used to express the theme of the delicacy and impermanence of the world in which we live, expressing a need for extreme care in the way we treat our environment. Flowers are symbols of the beauty of the world, and at the same time, its easy deterioration. They, along with other symbols of nature, have been used to make a stand against opposing ideologies present in the world, such as consumerism.

In this service, I decided to bring these two themes together. By creating an Interfaith ceremony I hope to highlight that many of the world's faiths (particularly those present in Britain) use flower symbolism. In order to do this, the main part of the service involves a member of each community offering a symbol with flower connections to the whole group, these shall become a symbol of our unity and alliance in caring for the world. Being the opening service of an Interfaith ecological centre, I hope this will illustrate some of the ecological symbolism found in flowers.

The Service

A Note on Text

Italics............	one person is speaking
Bold and ***Italics***...	*all present may say the words*
Bold..............	instructions
Normal............	information

The chairs have been arranged in a circle, to symbolise equality, unity, and the shape of the world in which we all live. The words 'Religious People Meeting Together(1) for the Sake of Our Earth' are written in roses on a colourful backdrop of marigolds.(2)
As all process in from the reception room, **these words may be said by all:**

We come together to this place, in a spirit of respect for religious differences, to try to bring our shared religious concerns for the welfare of our planet into realistic effective action.

Introductory drama - Local young people's dramatic society performs a short play entitled Wilful Destruction? Young children represent different species of plants, they act out the lives of the plants. The seed germinates and begins to grow; it breaks through the soil, produces leaves and flowers, the flower dies leaving a seed for new life. Children dressed as animals also come to eat the leaves from the plant. However as the new seed begins its cycle, more children (some in card-board cars, some in home-made buildings, some in paper chimneys), come to break the seed's cycle and take away its life. The animals have no food, they begin to disappear. The children who had destroyed the plant mourn for its loss, they plant new seeds and water them until they grow into new plants and they care for the animals.

The drama shows that although we have destroyed much nature and wildlife, we can, to some extent, undo what we have done.

Welcome, Presenter speaks - Speaker 1 (Each section of the ceremony would be spoken by a different individual, preferably speakers will be people in leadership roles within the individual communities.)

We welcome everyone here today for this special day of celebration and dedication of our new Interfaith Centre, which has been created for the education and advancement of care for the environment. We welcome the representatives of the Baha'i community, the Buddhist representatives, the members of the Christian community, the Hindu representatives, those from the Humanist movement, those from the faith of Islam, those representing the Jain faith, the Jewish representatives, the Sikh representatives and any others **(add here or delete as necessary.)** *We also welcome members of the conservation and environmental action groups who are here with us today.*

Introduction to the purpose of the centre - Speaker 2

As members of the world community we have come together to acknowledge our responsibility for the welfare of the planet in which we live and to make a stand against the systematic destruction of our environment; our Mother Earth. At Assisi in September 1986, each of the major faiths proclaimed through liturgy, Scripture, symbol and Declarations, their views on the issue of conservation. From this came the Network on Conservation and Religion which was established to assist in the development of partnership between conservation groups (such as the World Wildlife Fund) and religious communities world-wide. We hope to work on similar principles as the Network and learn from their experiences. However, we feel there is a need to have a centre here in Britain, created by the religious communities in Britain, working towards conservation and environmental protection in Britain. The centre is much more localised than the Network was. Finance shall be generated by our own communities here in Britain. It is our greatest hope, that this centre will become a beating heart for religious reflection on the state of our environment, and a springboard for action and education. I would now like to use a quote from Father Serrini from his introduction at Assisi:

> *We are convinced of the inestimable value of our respective traditions and of what they can offer to re-establish ecological harmony; but, at the same time, we are humble enough to desire to learn from each other. The very richness of our diversity lends strength to our shared concern and responsibility for our Planet Earth. (3)*

Introduction to the theme of the ceremony - Speaker 3

Flowers are a symbol of the beauty of the world, but they also remind us of its easy deterioration. It is for this reason that we have, here in the centre of the room, a model of the world, decorated in petals. These petals have been collected from our grounds, they have fallen from the plants, and will soon return to the ground as compost. Flowers naturally die and deteriorate, without doing so new life would not be possible. Although this process is natural in nature, human beings have brought about the early death of much of the world's wildlife and plant life, and we have not replaced it. We have created technology to 'control' nature and serve human greed, we have polluted our life-sustaining air, we have poisoned our water, we have devastated forests, not only is the beauty of the natural environment being destroyed, but its capacity to sustain life is under threat. We have come together because we recognise the fact that we need to reassess some of the values in Western society, and draw upon our religious traditions to help us once again value our world.

As a sign of our dedication to the future we have brought flower related symbols from our respective religions which show our admiration of the natural world and our dedication to caring for it. These objects are all items that will last the test of time, being living plants or made from durable materials. We hope that these signs will become reminders for us of our covenant here today. In order that they remain a constant symbol, after the service, they shall all be taken back to our places of worship.

Presenting of symbols from the various religious communities

Speaker 4 - We come together now to present our offerings as a sign of our alliance and unity in caring for our world. As each bring their offering, they may say a few words of explanation, and a reading or prayer of some sort. After the prayer or reading the representative will say, 'This is our offering', and we shall all respond with:

'This is our offering, we are united in caring for the world in which we live, as each petal takes its perfect form, we shall cradle it.'

We begin with the Baha'i faith - *The Baha'i House of Worship in India is in the shape of a Lotus, representing something pure which rises out of the dross of the world. The building has nine entrances which are equally spaced around the perimeter, representing an open door to all peoples, a place of common worship. Today we have brought a photograph of the Baha'i House of worship in India. It illustrates how the Lotus is an extremely important symbol for the Baha'i faith.*

<u>The photo is placed on the table in the middle of the room</u>

We have brought a reading which expresses the perfection of nature, which we should not bring into chaos:

> *This nature is subjected to an absolute organisation, to determined laws, to a complete order and to a finished design, from which it will never depart - to such a degree, indeed, that if you look carefully and with keen sight, from the smallest invisible atom up to such large bodies of the world of existence as the globe of the sun or other great stars and luminous spheres, whether you regard their arrangement, their composition, their form or their movement, you will find that all are in the highest degree of*

organisation and are under one law from which they will never depart. (Abdu'l Baha, Some Answered Questions, Chap XLVI p.207)

This is our offering.

This is our offering, we are united in caring for the world in which we live, as each petal takes its perfect form, we shall cradle it.

Buddhism - *We have brought a miniature sculpture of a Bo Tree, it was under a Bo Tree that we believe the Buddha achieved enlightenment.   It is highly revered in Buddhism.*

The sculpture is placed on the table in the middle of the room

We have decided to read an extract from Thich Nhat Hanh's 'Earth Gathas' which highlight the Buddhist idea that in order to help the state of the environment we need to change our attitude.   No longer seeing the Earth as something separate from ourselves, but seeing everything as interconnected.   We need the Earth, and the Earth needs us:

Earth Gathas

*The green Earth
is a miracle!
Walking in full awareness,
the wondrous Dharakaya is revealed.*

*Water flows from the high mountains.
Water runs deep in the Earth.
Miraculously, water comes to us
and sustains all life.*

*Garbage becomes rose.
Rose becomes compost
Everything is in transformation.
Even permanence is impermanent.*

*Dear plant, do not think you are alone.
This stream of water comes from Earth and sky.
The water is the Earth.
We are together for countless lives.*

*I entrust myself to Buddha;
Buddha entrusts himself to me.
I entrust myself to Earth;
Earth entrusts herself to me* [Nhat Hanh] © Parallax Press (4)

This is our offering

This is our offering, we are united in caring for the world in which we live, as each petal takes its perfect form, we shall cradle it.

Christianity - *We have brought a living white lily plant, the white lily has been a special symbol in Christianity for many years. It stands for purity, Mary the Mother of Jesus is often associated with white lilies due to her purity and virginity.*

The plant is placed on the table in the middle of the room

Traditionally Christianity has been criticised for encouraging an arrogant view towards nature. However, we believe this is being changed, as Christians become aware of what we are doing to the gift from God. This is expressed in a verse from a simple, yet poignant children's song. It is followed by a traditional song used at harvest time. They are sung for us today by some young Christians from the local Churches:

Think of a world

Part I

I Think of a world without any flowers,
Think of a world without any trees,
Think of a sky without any sunshine,
Think of the air without any breeze.
We thank you, Lord, for flowers and trees and sunshine
We thank you Lord, and praise your Holy Name. [Doreen Newport]

© 1969 Stainer and Bell Ltd, London, England

We Plough the Fields

*We plough the fields and scatter
the good seed on the land,
but it is fed and watered by God's almighty hand;
He sends the snow in winter,
the warmth to swell the grain,
the breezes and the sunshine
and soft refreshing rain.*

> *All good gifts around us are sent from heaven above,
> then thank the Lord, O thank the Lord,
> For all His love.*

*We thank You then, O Father,
for all things bright and good,
the seed-time and the harvest,
our life, our health, our food.
Accept the gifts we offer
for all Your love imparts;
we come now, Lord, to give You
our humble, thankful hearts.* [M.Claudius - Tr. J.M. Campbell]

This is our offering.

This is our offering, we are united in caring for the world in which we live, as each petal takes its perfect form, we shall cradle it.

Hinduism - 'We have brought a stylised picture of a Red Lotus Flower. This is a frequent and important symbol in Indian art and worship. The lotus is symbolic because it is something beautiful from something dirty. This shows that humans are masters of circumstances - you are what you make yourself. This is what the lotus explains, humans can come from "murky" circumstances, but still can achieve great things. You are what you make yourself'(5)

The picture is placed on the table in the middle of the room

The reading we have brought is used in devotion, which highlights the high regard we have for nature, it also features lotus and other flower symbolism.

You are the forest

you are all the great trees
in the forest

you are bird and beast
playing in and out
of all the trees

O lord white as jasmine
filling and filled by all

why don't you
show me your face ?

Would a circling surface vulture
know such depths of sky
as the moon would know ?

Would a weed in the riverbank
know such depths of water
as the lotus would know ?

Would a fly darting nearby
know the smell of flowers
as the bees would know ?

O lord white as jasmine
only you would know
the way of your devotees:
how would these,

these
mosquitoes
on the buffalo's hide ? [From Mahedeviyakka, Speaking of Siva] (7)

This reading shows the enormous impact that the natural world has had on Hinduism. The passage has great ecological significance, if Siva is in the trees and the animals how dare we destroy them ?

This is our offering

This is our offering, we are united in caring for the world in which we live, as each petal takes its perfect form, we shall cradle it.

Islam - *Islam particularly honours the Rose as a special flower, so we have brought a Rose Bush. Some say that the rose was created by a drop of perspiration which fell from Mohammed's [S] (7) forehead during His heavenly journey. The prophet himself is said to have been very fond of roses. The rose is perfect, and the true representative of everything spiritual. It reveals the beauty of the divine face which is immortal and will never perish.*

The Rose Bush is placed on the table in the middle of the room

Not only the rose is important in Islam, plants, trees and flowers are appreciated to the extent that Paradise is seen as a garden. We believe that we should care for nature as it's beauty represents and praises Allah. We would like to read a poem by Yunus, a medieval mystic who describes Paradise like this :

> *The rivers all in Paradise*
> *Flow with the word Allah, Allah,*
> *The branches of the Tuba Tree*
> *the tongue reciting the Qu'ran,*
> *the roses there in Paradise*
> *their fragrance is Allah, Allah. (8)*

This poem uses common Islamic symbolism to describe Paradise. Within, everything flows with praise for Allah, including trees and roses. The ecological significance is clear, if plants and wildlife are capable of giving praise to Allah, how can we destroy them without good reason ?

This is our offering

This is our offering, we are united in caring for the world in which we live, as each petal takes its perfect form, we shall cradle it.

Judaism - *We have brought an embroidery of some almond tree blossom. This is a symbol of the Jewish New Year for trees. Traditionally when the almond trees blossomed, was a time when tithes were presented to God. This is a symbol of giving the best of what you have been given from God, back to Him.*

The embroidery is placed on the table in the middle of the room

We will now read a prayer which is used at a special tree planting ceremony, it promotes caring for trees and acknowledges conservation as a religious duty:

> *Give dew for a blessing*
> *and cause beneficent rains to fall in their season*
> *To satiate the mountains of Israel and her valleys*
> *And to water thereon every plant and tree*
> *And these saplings*

Which we plant before this day.
Make deep their roots and wide their crown
Amongst all trees of Israel
for good and for beauty. (9)

This is our offering

This is our offering, we are united in caring for the world in which we live, as each petal takes its perfect form, we shall cradle it.

Sikhism - *We could not decide which flowers or plant we would like to represent our dedication to caring for our world. For this reason we have brought a painting depicting an image from our holy scripture the Guru Granth Sahib which shows the high regard we have for plant life and the fact that for Sikhs, as for many of us here today, conservation is a religious duty. The sentence I am to read briefly tells the story contained in the picture :*

Flower girl plucking petals, know in each
petal abides life. (Guru Granth Sahib p.479)

The painting is placed on the table in the middle of the room.

The reading we have brought shows how we proclaim the glory of God in nature. It is taken from the Guru Granth Sahib (p.463), and expresses the Sikh belief that God is seated in Nature, and His spirit is continuously present within it. This feeling of utmost respect for nature makes conservation a religious duty for many Sikhs. We feel that God intended us to maintain and care for his creation, this can be achieved by ethical behaviour :

In Nature we see God,
in Nature we hear his speech;
Nature inspires devotional reveries.
In nature is the essence of joy and peace.
Earth, sky, nether regions comprise Nature.
The whole creation is an embodiment of Nature.
Air, water, fire, earth, dust are all parts of Nature,
the Omnipotent Creator commands, observes and
pervades Nature. (10)

This is our offering

This is our offering, we are united in caring for the world in which we live, as each petal takes its perfect form, we shall cradle it.

A short address, Speaker 5 -

As we come to the end of this our opening ceremony, we remember the symbol of flowers which we began with, we remember how as flowers are a symbol for the beauty of the world, they also remind us of its easy deterioration. We know that when we try to grow house plants, without very careful tending, they can easily die. This theme is exemplified in a poem by Robert Herrick, an English poet who lived from 1591-1674:

To Daffodils

Fair daffodils, we weep to see
*   You haste away so soon;*
As yet the early rising sun
*   Has not attained his noon.*
*   Stay, stay,*
*   Until the hasting day*
*   Has run*
*   But to the evensong;*
And having pray'd together, we
*   Will go with you along.*

We have short time to stay, as you,
*   We have as short a spring;*
As quick a growth to meet decay,
*   As you, or anything.*
*   We die,*
*   As your hours do, and dry*
*   Away,*
*   Like to the summer's rain;*
Or as the pearl's of morning's dew,
*   Ne'er to be found again.*

This poem was used during a course I undertook at Westminster College, Oxford, named 'The Culture of Flowers'. I feel it can be interpreted to explain exactly what we want to show in the symbolism of the flowers in this service. It identifies our short lives with that of the daffodils, as they die, we die. This reminds us that we are all part of nature, and all part of the same world. For myself it carries a deep ecological message; we need to shift our attitude from one that looks upon the natural world as separate and inferior, to one which sees everything around ourselves as special, and as such essential to our very being.

We need to realise that our actions have an effect on the world around us, if we continue to rape the world, it will eventually cease to be. The Earth's resources are not unlimited - so it is important to recognise that everything we do has an impact. These sentiments have been expressed through the ages. Over a hundred years ago Chief Seattle uttered these profound words of wisdom:

This we know
The Earth does not belong to man;
This we know
All things are connected
like the blood which unites one family.
All things are connected.

Whatever befalls the Earth
befalls the sons of the Earth.
Man did not weave the web of life,
he is merely a strand in it.
Whatever he does to the web,
he does to himself. (11) © Parallax Press.

All of the religions represented here today have invaluable teachings and knowledge that can help us in our mutual struggle.   With the aid of our inheritance we can work together to care for the world in which we all live.   A world which for some of us is seen as God-given and as such special and holy, a world which for others among us is seen as part of everything that we are.   Whichever world-view we belong to, we all now recognise the need to care for the Planet Earth.   So, let us unite, look towards our table of offerings and say these words together :

All: **This is our offering, we are united in caring for the world in which we live, as each petal takes its perfect form, we shall cradle it.   Let these objects become for us a sign of our commitment and dedication to the world.   No longer will we damage the Earth.**

A short prayer will now be offered by a representative from each of the faiths present, followed by silence for individual contemplation.   We shall then move to the grounds for the tree planting.   Each world-view represented has brought a young tree to be planted in the grounds of the new centre, plants are also welcome.   This allows us to show practically how we can help the environment.

Excerpts from *Dharma Gaia: A harvest of Essays in Buddhism and Ecology*, edited by Alan Hunt Badiner, are reprinted with permission of Parallax Press, Berkeley, California.

INTERFAITH WORSHIP SERVICE

ONLY ONE EARTH

A SERVICE HONOURING OUR HOLY MOTHER EARTH

SAINT BENEDICT CENTER, MADISON, WISCONSIN
APRIL 23, 1995,

ORDER OF WORSHIP

PROCESSIONAL

[Members of the Interfaith Dialogue Group bring symbols of their faiths into the chapel and place them on the altar.   They then take seats reserved for them at the ends of nearby rows.]

RECORDING: Spring Morning Songs: Wisconsin woodland and meadow birds.

PHOTO BACKDROP: NASA, Apollo 7: The Earth from space.

HYMN   [CONGREGATION STANDING]

Morning Has Broken
                                                                                    BUNESSAN
                                                                    Robert LeBlanc, organ

Morning has broken
Like the first morning;
Blackbird has spoken
Like the first bird.
Praise for the singing!
Praise for the morning!
Praise for them, springing
Fresh from the Word!

Sweet the rain's new fall
Sunlit from heaven
Like the first dewfall
On the first grass.
Praise for the sweetness
Of the wet garden
Sprung in completeness
Where his feet pass

Mine is the sunlight!
Mine is the morning
Born of the one light
Eden saw play!
Praise with elation,
Praise every morning,
God's re-creation
Of the new Day!

                                                                        Eleanor Farjeon
© Reprinted with permission of David Higham Associates from *The Childrens Bells*, OUP.

INTRODUCTION AND WELCOME

                                                                        Ken Smits
                                                                        Eunice Chagnon

CALL TO WORSHIP

L   From you, O Divine Mystery, has emerged the evolving universe, and the whole creation is full of your glory.

C   We are part of this wondrous universe and members of the Great Community of Life on Planet Earth.

L   Open your hearts to the miracle of being and the Divine Presence.

C   We open our hearts and give thanks for the gift of life and for our home on Planet Earth.

L   The light of God surrounds you;
The love of God enfolds you;
The power of God protects you;
The presence of God watches over you.
Wherever you are, God is!

CHANTS FROM SACRED TEXTS

HINDU   Bala Kale, Amalendu & Sujata Bagchi, Swapna Chowdhuri

[A conch shell is blown to purify the space]

Truth, cosmic order, consecration, austerity, prayer and holy sacrifice: these uphold the earth. May she, the ruling mistress of what has been and what will be, prepare for us a wide and limitless abode.

Whether we stand upright or sit, whether we stay quite still or walk, and whether we start with right foot or left, may we never falter upon the Earth.

O purifying Earth, I invoke you! O patient Earth, bearer of nourishment and strength, of bread and butter; O earth, by sacred word enhanced, we approach you with the praise due to you.

The Earth carries in her lap the foolish and the wise. She bears the death of the wicked as well as the good. She lives in friendly collaboration with the tame pig and offers herself as sanctuary to the wild boar.

O Earth, O Mother, be gracious to me that I may be at ease, O Earth, O Poet, wth grace and good fortune set me in harmony with all the divine powers.
- from the Bhumi Sukta (Atharvaveda, XII, 1, 1-63).

May there be peace in the heavens, peace in the skies, and peace on earth. May the waters be peaceful. May the grasses and herbs bring peace to all creatures, and may the plants be at peace also. May the beneficent beings bring us peace, and may the way of all creation bring peace throughout the world. May all things be peaceful, and may that peace itself bring further peace. May we also bring peace to all.
Yajurveda, 36,17

HYMN [CONGREGATION STANDING]

For the Beauty of the Earth
DIX
Robert LeBlanc, organ

For the beauty of the earth,
For the beauty of the skies,
For the love which from our birth
Over and around us lies:

Gracious God, to thee we raise
This our sacrifice of praise.

For the beauty of each hour
of the day and of the night,
Hill and vale, and tree and flower,
Sun and moon and stars of light:

For the joy of ear and eye,
For the heart and mind's delight,
For the mystic harmony
Linking sense to sound and sight:

For the joy of human love,
Brother, sister, parent, child,
Friends on earth, and friends above,
Pleasures pure and undefiled:

For each perfect gift of thine
To our race so freely given,
Graces human and divine,
Flowers of earth and buds of heaven:

READINGS FROM SACRED TEXTS

JEWISH
Daniel Pakarsky

But the land which you are going over to possess is a land of hills and valleys, which drinks water by the rain from heaven, a land which the Lord your God cares for; the eyes of the Lord your God are always upon it, from the beginning of the year to the end of the year. And if you will obey my commandments which I command you this day, to love the Lord your God, and to serve him with all your heart and with all your soul, he will give the rain for your land in its season, the early rain, and the later rain, that you may gather in your grain and your wine and your oil. And he will give grass in your fields for your cattle, and you shall eat and be full.

- Torah, Deuteronomy, 11:11-15

PSALM

Marie Stephen Reges

You stretch the heavens out like a tent,
you build your palace on the waters above;
using the clouds as your chariot,
you advance on the wings of the wind;
you use the winds as messengers
and fiery flames as servants.

You fixed the earth on its foundations,
unshakeable for ever and ever;
you wrapped it with the deep as with a robe,
the waters overtopping the mountains.

At your reproof the waters took to flight,
they fled at the sound of your thunder,
cascading over the mountains, into the valleys,
down to the reservoir you made for them;
you imposed the limits they must never cross again,
or they would once more flood the land.

The trees of the Lord get rain enough,
those cedars of Lebanon he planted;
here the little birds build their nest
and, on the highest branches, the stork has its home.
For the wild goats there are the mountains,
in the crags the badgers hide.

You made the moon to tell the seasons,
the sun knows when to set.

All creatures depend on you
to feed them throughout the year;
you provide the food they eat,
with generous hand you satisfy their hunger.

I mean to sing to the Lord all my life,
I mean to play for my God as long as I live.

- Psalm 104, 3-9, 16-19. 37-28, 33.

EASTERN ORTHODOX CHRISTIAN

John-Brian Paprock

Bless the Lord, O my soul;
Blessed art Thou, Lord.
O Lord, my God, Thou art very great;
Blessed art Thou, O Lord.
How marvellous are Thy works, O Lord,
Thou has made all things in wisdom;
Glory to Thee, O Lord, who has made them all.
Glory to the Father, and to the Son, and to the Holy Spirit, now and ever,
and to ages of ages.   Amen
Alleluia, Glory to Thee, O God.

from vespers hymn, 'Bless the Lord'

SONGS FROM THE FAMILY OF CREATION

[Readers rise but stay at their places to read these texts; they do not speak from the lectern.]

Eskimo Woman Shaman, quoted by Rasmussen   Dawn Shegonee

> The great sea
> Has sent me adrift,
> It moves me as the weed in a great river,
> Earth and the great weather move me,
> Have carried me away,
> And move my inward parts with joy.

SENG-T'SAN   George Hinger

> One thing is all, all things are one -
> Know this and all is whole and complete.

BLACK ELK   Art Shegonee

> I was seeing in a sacred manner the shapes of all things in the spirit, and the
> shape of all shapes as they must live together like one being.   And I saw that
> the sacred hoop of my people was one of many hoops that made one circle,
> wide as daylight and as starlight, and in the centre grew one mighty flowering
> tree to shelter all the children of one mother and one father.   And I saw that it
> was holy.

GERALD MANLEY HOPKINS   Audrey Hinger

> Glory be to God for dappled things -
>   For skies of couple-colour as a brinded cow;
>   for rose-moles all in stipple upon trout that swim;
> Fresh-firecoal chestnut-falls; finches' wings;
>   Landscape plotted and pieced - fold, fallow, and plough;
>   And áll trádes, their gear and tackle and trim.
> All things counter, original, spare, strange;
>   Whatever is fickle, freckled (who knows how?)
>   With swift, slow; sweet, sour; adazzle, dim;
> He fathers-forth whose beauty is past change:
>   Praise him.

DEVARA DASIMAYYA   Daniel Gómez-Ibáñez

> Whatever It was
>
> that made this earth
> the base,
> the world its life,
> the wind its pillar,
> arranged the lotus and the moon,
> and covered it all with folds
> of sky
>
> with Itself inside.

to that Mystery
indifferent to differences,
to It I pray,
O Ramanatha.

ADRIENNE RICH   Georgia Gómez-Ibáñez

My heart is moved by all I cannot save:
so much has been destroyed.

I have to cast my lot with those
who age after age, perversely,

with no extraordinary power,
reconstitute the world.

SOLO   HUMPBACK WHALE NEAR BERMUDA

READINGS FROM SACRED TEXTS

MUSLIM   Nabil Maalej

And it is he who spread out the earth, and set thereon Mountains standing firm, and (flowing) rivers: and fruit of every kind he made in pairs, two and two: He draweth the night as a veil over the day.   Behold verily in these things there are signs for those who consider!.   And in the earth are tracts (diverse though) neighbouring, and gardens of vines and fields sown with corn, and palm trees growing out of single roots or otherwise: watered with the same water, yet some of them we make more excellent than others to eat.   Behold, verily in these things there are signs for those who understand.

Assuredly the creation of the heavens
And the earth is greater
Than the creation of mankind;
Yet most of mankind understands not.

- translations from the Qu'ran, XIII: 3-4; XL:57

BAHA'I   Paul & Ellie Jacobi

Reflect upon the inner realities of the universe, the secret wisdoms involved, the enigmas, the interrelationships, the rules that govern all.   For every part of the universe is connected with every other part by ties that are very powerful and admit of no imbalance, nor any slackening whatever .....   Even as the human body in this world, which is outwardly composed of different limbs and organs, is in reality a closely integrated, coherent entity, similarly the structure of the physical world is like unto a single being whose limbs and members are inseparably linked together.   Become clear that the greatest relationship that bindeth the world of being together lieth in the range of created things themselves, and that cooperation, mutual aid, and reciprocity are essential characteristics in the unified body of the world of being, inasmuch as all created things are closely related together and each is influenced by the other or deriveth benefit therefrom, either directly or indirectly.

- 'Abdu'l Baha

RESPONSIVE READING

[The leaders read from the four corners of the chapel: East from the eastern corner, South from left of the entrance, West from the western corner, North from the lectern, and Earth from the center. Leaders should take their positions before they need to begin reading, so there are no pauses in the prayer.]

PRAYER TO THE FOUR WINDS

THE EAST
John-Brian Paprock

L We greet you, O Spirit of the East. You usher in the dawn on your breeze; you stretch forth your fingers and paint our skies.

C Awaken in us with each new day, new hopes, new dreams of colours, love and joys never before imagined.

L. Fill our bodies with your breath; invigorate us. Carry us to the farthest mountains and beyond.

C In-spirit us that we might reach out to you boldly to grasp the miracles that are given birth with each new dawn.

THE SOUTH
Bibi Bagchi

L We greet you, Spirit of the South. You bring the winds of summer and breathe on us the warmth of the sun to soothe and heal our bodies and our spirits.

C You thaw and soften the coldness of our world; you nudge the seedlings to break through the soil to light.

L Quicken us, draw us by the urgings of your warm breath to break through the soil of our own barrenness and fear.

C Drive our roots deep into the earth and stretch our branches full out into the sky.

L Teach us to hold sacred the memory of the spring rains that we might have the strength to withstand the heat of the day, and not become parched and narrow in our love.

C Lead us to accept fatigue with resignation, knowing that life is not to be rushed, that there is no flower of the field that grows from seed to blossoms in a single day.

THE WEST
Eunice Chagnon

L We greet you, Spirit of the West.

C You cool our hot tired bodies, refresh and bring laughter to our hearts. It is you who usher in the setting sun.

L It is by your power that the sun hangs suspended for endless moments before you catch it with your breath and carry it off into the night.

C Guide our steps at the end of the day; keep us safe from evil. Fill us with your peace as you enfold us with your great mystery of night that we might rest securely in your arms until morning calls us forth again.

THE NORTH
Peter Brinkman

L   We greet you, Spirit of the North. You are the cold, biting wind that blows across our land, that strips the earth of all that is dead and decayed, that robs us of the false securities, so easily blown away.

C   Teach us to plant our feet securely on the earth and to see things as they really are, that the coming of your spirit may find us standing firm in integrity.

L   It is your Spirit whose winds bring the snows of winter, with their fury and their solitude. It is your Spirit who blankets the earth for sleep.

C   Teach us, Spirit of the North, in the solitude of winter, to wait in darkness with the sleeping earth, believing that we, like the earth, already hold within ourselves the seeds of new life.

THE EARTH
Dawn Shegonee

L   We greet you, Great Spirit of the Earth.

C   It was from you we came as from a Mother; you nourish us still and give us shelter.

L   Teach us to walk softly on your lands, to use with care your gifts, to love with tenderness all our brothers and sisters who have been born of your goodness.

C   And when the day comes you call us back to yourself, help us to return to you as a friend, to find ourselves embraced, encircled, enfolded in your arms.

OFFERING OF THE FOUR ELEMENTS: EARTH, AIR , FIRE, WATER.

[CONGREGATION SEATED]

[The elements are brought one after the other by the readers from the four corners of the chapel and placed on the central table. First, earth (a pot of flowers) is brought from the east by John-Brian Paprock, then Dini Dutta brings fire (a candle) from the south, Eunice Chagnon brings water from the west, and last, Peter Brinkman brings air(incense) from the North. While these offerings are made, George Hinger invites a bell to sound.

After the incense has been placed on the table and as the sound of the bell dies away, Georgia Gómez-Ibáñez recites the Zuni prayer.]

RECITATION
Georgia Gómez-Ibáñez

[from a Zuni offering prayer]

> This is what I want to happen: that our earth mother
> may be clothed in ground corn four times over;
> that frost flowers cover her over entirely;
> that the mountain pines far away over there
> may stand close to each other in the cold;
> that the weight of snow crack some branches!
> In order that the country may be this way
> I have made my prayer sticks into something alive.

- (tr. Robert Bly)

REFLECTION

CHRISTIAN SCIENCE   George Hinger, for Martha Kilgour

What a amazing paradox it is to realise that what happens to a remote area of a country like Brazil can have an effect upon the entire world.   Such a fact hints at a deeper, spiritual truth: our prayers, no matter how remote they may seem from the mainstream of busy lives, have the power to uplift and transform the hearts of men and women all over the world.

- Christian Science Sentinel, May 14, 1990.

READINGS FROM RELIGIOUS TEXTS

BUDDHIST   Sharpa Tulku
[translated from Tibetan]

May there abound in all directions
Gardens of wish-fulfilling trees
Filled with the sweet sound of Wisdom
Proclaimed by the Holy Beings.

And may the earth everywhere be pure,
Smooth and devoid of rough terrains,
Level like the palm of the hand,
And of the nature of lapis lazuli.

For as long as space endures,
And for as long as living beings remain,
Until then may I too abide to dispel the misery of the world.

Shantideva: Guide to the Bodhisattva's Way of Life, 10: 34.35.55

SILENT MEDITATION

Introduced by Polly Wood

Five minutes of silence.   Afterwards, individuals may feel moved to say something to the congregation.

PRAYER OF RECONCILIATION

[READ IN UNISON]
[CONGREGATION REMAIN SEATED]

We humbly acknowledge that the integrity of Creation has been disrupted by the ways we have chosen to live.   We have been more concerned with our private happiness than with the well-being of the larger community of life.   In this we have been short-sighted, ignoring the teachings of science.   In this we have been hard-hearted, not caring about the suffering of our fellow human beings and other life forms and forgetting the needs of future generations.   We have become confused about the moral values which should guide our lives;   we have lost our spiritual center.

We pledge ourselves to overcome our ignorance, to discipline our careless desires, and to purge our hearts of hatred in obedience to the spirit of truth, goodness, and peace.

SONGS FROM THE FAMILY OF CREATION

RUMI   Peter Brinkman

Out beyond ideas of wrongdoing and rightdoing,
there is a field.   I'll meet you there.

When the soul lies down in that grass,
the world is too full to talk about.
Ideas, language, even the phrase each other
doesn't make any sense.

FROM THE NAVAJO BLESSINGWAY   Georgia Gómez-Ibáñez

Before me, beauty
Behind me, beauty
Below me, beauty
Above me, beauty
Around me , beauty
May I speak beauty
May I walk in beauty always
Beauty I am.
All is restored to beauty,
All is restored to beauty,
All is restored to beauty,
All is restored to beauty.

Wolf Eyes   RECORDING: PAUL WINTER CONSORT

BENEDICTION   Daniel Gómez-Ibáñez

God makes the rivers to flow.   They tire not, nor do they cease from flowing.

May the river of my life flow into the sea of love that is the Lord.   May I overcome all the
impediments in my course.   May the thread of my song be not cut before my life merges in
the sea of love.

Guard me against all danger, O Lord.   Accept me graciously, O King of kings.

Release me from my sorrows, which hold me as ropes hold a calf.   I cannot even open my
eyes without the power of your love.

Guard us against the grief that haunts the life of the selfish.   Lead us from darkness into light.

We will sing of your love as it was sung of old.   Your laws change not, but stand like
mountains.

Forgive me all the mistakes I have committed. Many mornings will dawn upon us again.
Guide us through them all, O lord of love.

- Rg Veda,II, 28:4-9

RECESSIONAL
Joyful, we hail this glorious day   JOHANN GOTTFRIED WALTHER

PRAYER

for Victims of Land Mines

NOTRE DAME DE BON SECOURS
BRUSSELS

24 JUNE 1997

THE HUMAN FAMILY

BAHA'I
 Blessed is he who preferreth his brother before himself. - Baha'u'llah, Tablets of Baha'ullah, 71

BUDDHISM
 A state which is not pleasant or enjoyable for me will also not be so for him; and how can I impose on another a state which is not pleasant or enjoyable for me ? - Samyutta Nikaya, V

CHRISTIANITY:
 All things whatsoever ye would that men should do to you, do ye even so to them. - Matthew 7.12.

CONFUCIANISM:
 Do not unto others what you would not have them do unto you. - Analects 15:23

HINDUISM:
 This is the sum of duty: do naught unto others which would cause you pain if done to you. - Mahabharata, XIII:114

ISLAM:
 No one of you is a believer until he desires for his brother that which he desires for himself. - an-Nawawi, 40 Hadith, 13

JAINISM:
 In happiness and suffering, in joy and grief, we should regard all creatures as we regard our own self. - Mahavira

JUDAISM:
 What is hateful to you, do not to your fellow man.   That is the law: all the rest is commentary. - Talmud, Shabbat 31a

NATIVE AMERICAN:
 Respect for life is the foundation. - The Great Law of Peace

SIKHISM:
 Don't create enmity with anyone as God is within everyone. - Guru Arjan Devji 258, Guru Granth Sahib

ZOROASTRIANISM:
 That nature only is good when it shall not do unto another whatever is not good for its own self. - Dadistan-i-Dinik, 94.5

VEDIC PEACE MANTRAS

J'AI DEUX ENFANTS. J'AI ÉTÉ BLESSÉE PAR UNE MINE EN 1991 PENDANT QUE JE CHERCHAIS DU BOIS POUR LE FEU - NOTRE FAMILLE VIT GRÂCE À LA VENTE DU BOIS POUR CHAUFFER LE SUCRE DE PALME. APRÈS AVOIR PERDU MA JAMBE, J'AI EU DES PROBLÈMES AVEC MA FAMILLE PARCE QUE JE NE POUVAIS PLUS TRAVAILLER. MON MARI VIT AVEC MOI MAIS IL EST ABSENT PENDANT DE LONGUES PÉRIODES. JE NE SAIS PAS OÙ IL VA. IL SE FÂCHE SOUVENT. JE NE PEUX FAIRE QUE DES TRAVAUX LÉGERS; ALORS QUAND IL EST ABSENT JE N'ARRIVE PAS À FAIRE TOUT-CE QU'IL FAUT POUR LA FAMILLE. AU CONTAIRE, JE SUIS UNE LOURDE CHARGE POUR EUX. MES ENFANTS ONT CINQ ET TROIS ANS. MA FAMILLE A BESOIN DE MON TRAVAIL TOUS LES JOURS. MAIS MAINTENANT JE DEVIENS DE PLUS EN PLUS PAUVRE À CAUSE DE CETTE MINE.
- UNE FEMME CAMBODGIENNE

Om. May the circumstances of all beings be auspicious. May all beings enjoy peace. May all be full and may all prosper and be happy and free from disease. May all strive to be kind to others. May none despair.

Om. Lead me from the unreal to the real, from darkness to life, from death to immortality. May Mitra, Varuna and Aryama be good to us. May Indra and Brihaspati and Vishnu of great strides be good to us. Prostrations to Brahman.

Prostrations to Thee, O Vayu, who art the visible Brahman. I shall call Thee the Just and the True. May he protect the teacher and me. May he protect the teacher. *Om*. Peace, Peace, Peace.

Om. May He protect us both (teacher and student). May we find true freedom. May we grow in strength together and live by the true light of the scriptures. May our studies together be fruitful. May we never quarrel.

Om. Peace, Peace, Peace. May He, the Lord of all, pre-eminent among the Vedas and superior to the nectar contained in them, bless me with wisdom. May I be adorned with knowledge of Brahman that leads to Immortality. May my body become strong and vigorous (for practicing meditation on Brahman). May my tongue always utter delightful words. May I hear fully with my ears. Thou art the scabbard of Brahman, hidden by worldly taints (and not revealed by puny intellects.) May I never forget that which I have learned. *Om*. Peace, Peace, Peace.

I am the destroyer of the tree of Samsara (worldly tendencies). My reputation is as high as the mountain top. In essence I am as pure as the Sun. I am the highest treasure. I am immortal, indestructible. This is my realization. *Om*. Peace, Peace, Peace.

Om. That (Brahman) is full. This (this universe) is full. Fullness is born from fullness. If fullness is removed from fullness, fullness remains. *Om*. Peace, peace, peace.

May my limbs, speech, life-force, eye, ear, and the power of all my senses grow vigorous. All is Brahman of the Upanishads. May I never deny the Brahman. May the Brahman never desert me. Let that relationship endure. Let the virtues recited in the Upanishads be rooted in me. May they repose in me. *Om*. Peace, Peace, Peace.

Let my speech be rooted in my mind. Let my mind be rooted in my speech. Let Brahman reveal Himself to me. Let my mind and speech enable me to grasp the Truth of the Vedas. Let me remember all I have heard. Let me spend both day and night in study. I think Truth. I speak Truth. May that Truth protect me. May that which protects the teacher protect me. *Om*. Peace, Peace, Peace.

Om. O worshipful ones, may our ears hear what is auspicious. May we see what is auspicious. May we sing your praises, living our allotted span of life in perfect health and strength. May Indra extolled in the scriptures, Pushan the all-knowing, Tarkshya who saves us from all harm, and Brihaspati who protects our spiritual lustre, give us success in our study of the scriptures and the practice of the truths contained therein. *Om.* Peace, Peace, Peace.

Om. He who creates this universe in the beginning and He whom the Vedas gloriously praise, in Him I take refuge in the firm faith that my intellect may shine with the knowledge of Brahman. *Om.* Peace, Peace, Peace.

CLOSE TO THE MINEFIELDS THE SITUATION OF THE HUNGRY IS EVEN WORSE. THEY ARE OFTEN WILLING TO SCAVENGE IN THE MINEFIELD FOR FOOD OR FOR SOMETHING TO SELL TO BUY FOOD. SOME TYPES OF MINE CASING CAN BE SOLD FOR MOTOR BIKE SPARE PARTS, THEY TELL ME, BUT YOU HAVE TO GO IN THERE TO DISABLE THE MINE. SOMETIMES THE PARENTS OF A HUNGRY FAMILY CAN BE RECRUITED TO DO DANGEROUS OR VIOLENT ACTS. A SMALL AMOUNT OF MONEY CAN BUY THE SERVICES OF A VERY POOR MAN.

- CAMBODIAN VILLAGER

PRAYER & RESPONSES

READER: Today we pray specially for a world of peace, a world free to celebrate and dance, a world free from mines.
We pray for families who have members killed by land mines.

ALL: Comfort them.

READER: We pray for children, women and men struggling to build a new life.

ALL: Give them courage.

READER: We pray for a change of heart for the producers of land mines.

ALL: May they use their engineering and business skills for development, not war.

READER: We pray for the de-miners.

ALL: Grant them safety and perseverance in their holy work.

READER: We pray for countries severely afflicted by land mines.

ALL: May their lands be abundant with rice and corn and food, not desecrated by land mines.

READER: We pray for the heads of governments.

ALL: May they ban mines in Ottawa this December, and give funds for demining and for victim assistance.

READER: Dear God, thank you for your loving kindness. Forgive our faults, and help us to do good, not evil.

KARANIYAMETTA SUTTA

> WHAT IS MORE FLUID, MORE YIELDING THAN WATER? YET BACK IT COMES AGAIN, WEARING DOWN THE RIGID STRENGTH WHICH CANNOT YIELD TO WITHSTAND IT. SO IT IS THAT THE STRONG ARE OVERCOME BY THE WEAK, THE HAUGHTY BY THE HUMBLE. THIS WE KNOW, BUT NEVER LEARN
>
> *- LAO-TZU*

> WE WILL PRACTICE WHAT WE PROFESS.
>
> *- ZOROASTRIAN PRAYER*

The Discourse on loving-kindness:

This is what should be done by one skilled in good who would attain that state of peace: That person should be able, upright, truly straight and gentle and not proud, contented, easy to support, with few duties and frugal habits, calm in faculties and discreet, not puffed up, not greedy among lay-supporters. Let that person not do even the slightest thing which later on the wise might blame. One should contemplate thus: May all beings be happy and secure. Whatever living beings there are, weak or strong, omitting none, those which are long or great, middle-sized, short, subtle or gross, and those which are seen, or unseen, and those which dwell far or near, beings and spirits: may they all be happy! Let none deceive another, nor despise anyone at all, or with anger or thoughts of hate wish suffering for another. Thus as a mother guards her only child with her life, in the same way one should care for all beings. One's mind should develop loving-kindness for all the world, without limits. One's mind should extend above, below, and all around, unbounded, without malice or enmity. Standing or walking, sitting or lying down, one should remain alert and firmly mindful of this. This is Divine: abiding in the here and now, free from ignorance, not subject to narrow views, free from greed for sensual pleasures, virtuous and possessed of profound insight. This is the way that leads to Nirvana.

- Suttanipata: 1-8

MEDITATION

> THIS WORLD WAS NOT LEFT TO US BY OUR PARENTS, IT WAS LENT TO US BY OUR CHILDREN
>
> *- AFRICAN PROVERB*

Lord, how can I serve you without arms?
How can I walk in your way without feet?
I was collecting sticks for the fire when I lost my arms,
I was taking the goats to water when I lost my feet.
I have a head but my head does not understand why there are land mines in the grazing land or why there is a trip wire across the dusty road to the market.

My heart is filled with a long ache. I want to share your pain but I cannot. It is too deep for me. You look at me but I cannot bear your gaze. The arms factory provides a job for my son and my taxes paid for the development of 'smart' bombs. I did not protest when the soldiers planted fear into the earth that smothers the old people and the anxious mothers, and fills the young men with hate.

Lord, we are all accomplices in the crime of war which is a lust for power at all costs. The cost is too much for humanity to bear.

Lord, give us back our humanity, our *ubuntu*...
Teach us to serve you without arms, Amen

Desmond M. Tutu

AFFIRMATIONS I

READER: We think with compassion of all who have been bereaved, injured, or maimed by land mines.

ALL: May they find comfort.

READER: We think with compassion of communities divided by fear and hatred.

ALL: May they know peace.

READER: We think with gratitude of those who clear land mines and seek to ban them.

ALL: May they have courage.

> WE COMMIT OURSELVES TO A CULTURE OF NON-VIOLENCE, RESPECT, JUSTICE, AND PEACE.   WE SHALL NOT OPPRESS, INJURE, TORTURE, OR KILL OTHER HUMAN BEINGS, FORSAKING VIOLENCE AS A MEANS OF SETTLING DIFFERENCES ...
>
> WE INVITE ALL PEOPLE, WHETHER RELIGIOUS OR NOT, TO DO THE SAME.
> - *Towards a Global Ethic: An Initial Declaration signed by leaders from all the world's faith traditions, Parliament of the World's Religions, Chicago, 1993.*
>
> THE WORLD IN ARMS IS NOT SPENDING MONEY ALONE.
> IT IS SPENDING THE SWEAT OF ITS LABOURERS,
> THE GENIUS OF ITS SCIENTISTS,
> THE HOPES OF ITS CHILDREN.
> - DWIGHT D.EISENHOWER

PRAYER AND READING

Glory to God, creator of all,   It is he who gives us life, he who gives us death.   He is most high, omniscient.

God of creation, light of lights, created man to benefit from that light which is the mercy of the heavens and the earth.

God is the Peace that is a boon of Allah for all of humanity.   The Prophet (peace be upon him) said, 'A person's faith is expressed by three things: justice, charity, and peace.'

The believer prays, 'O God, you are Peace; lead us to your Paradise, the home of Peace.'

In this world of divisions, atrocities, and wars, may the innocent be spared.   Their hands are clean.   May their steps never find the minefields of death and mutilation.

May we be horrified and forever haunted by the images of children torn apart, fitted with protheses, or bedridden for life.   As long as humanity can even imagine such crimes, we call upon God to send us his justice and to protect us from evil.

God of all, ruler of humankind, protect us from evil, whether from humans or from the devil's temptation.

- Dr Dalil Boubakeur

QUR'AN: SURAH 1: THE SEVEN VERSES

1.   *In the name of Allah the all-merciful, most compassionate*

2.   *Praised be Allah, Lord of the universe,*

3.   *The all-merciful, most-compassionate,*

4.   *Lord of the day of judgment,*

5.   *It is you alone we adore, you alone are our succour,*

6.   *Show us the straight path,*

7.   *The path of those whom you have blessed, not the path of those who have incurred your wrath, nor the path of those who have strayed.*

MY HEART IS MOVED BY ALL I CANNOT SAVE: SO MUCH HAS BEEN DESTROYED I HAVE TO CAST MY LOT WITH THOSE WHO AGE AFTER AGE, PERVERSELY, WITH NO EXTRAORDINARY POWER, RECONSTITUTE THE WORLD

- Adrienne Rich

AFFIRMATIONS II

READER: We think of those who make and plant land mines.

ALL: May their consciences be awakened to what they do.

READER: We acknowledge the prejudice, greed, and lack of concern in our own hearts.

ALL: May we become aware of the sufferings of others.

READER: We recognize the failure of the nations to which we belong to seek peace and pursue it.

ALL: May we help awaken our nation to its urgent responsibility.

READER: We know that the religions of the world have been misused to foment violence and hatred.

ALL: May people of faith everywhere work together for understanding and peace.

WHATEVER GOD DOES, THE FIRST OUTBURST IS ALWAYS COMPASSION. - MEISTER ECKHART

> AND THEY SHALL BEAT THEIR SWORDS INTO PLOUGHSHARES.
> AND THEIR SPEARS INTO PRUNING HOOKS;
> NATION SHALL NOT LIFT UP SWORD AGAINST NATION,
> NEITHER SHALL THEY LEARN WAR ANY MORE;
> BUT THEY SHALL SIT EVERY ONE UNDER THE VINE
> AND UNDER THE TREE
> AND NONE SHALL MAKE THEM AFRAID
>
> *- Micah 4:3-4*

PRAYER FOR PEACE

May it be pleasing before Thee, Lord our God and God of our Mothers and Fathers.

To abolish wars and shedding of blood from the world.

And to extend a great and wondrous peace through the world.

No more shall nation lift up sword unto nation, and no more shall they learn war.

Only let all the dwellers on earth recognise and know the very truth:

That we have not come to this world for the sake of strife and division (God forbid)

Nor for the sake of hatred and envy, provocation and shedding of blood (God forbid)

Only we have come to the world in order to recognise and know Thee.

Be thou Blessed Forever .....

May the Scripture be fulfilled, as it is written:

And I will give peace in the land

And you shall lie down with none to make you tremble

And I will cause evil beasts to cease from the land

And the sword shall not pass through your land.

- Rabbi Nathan of Braslav: Likkutei Tefilot, 2, 53.

> OH GOD,
> YOU ARE PEACE
> FROM YOU COMES PEACE
> TO YOU RETURNS PEACE
> REVIVE US WITH A SALUTATION OF PEACE
> AND LEAD US TO YOUR ABODE OF PEACE.
> *Muslim daily prayer*

I SUPPORT THE INTERNATIONAL CAMPAIGN TO BAN LANDMINES. THE TERRIBLE TOLL THAT LANDMINES TAKE CLEARLY SHOWS THE IMMENSE DESTRUCTION AND SUFFERING THAT THESE AWFUL WEAPONS ARE CAPABLE OF CAUSING. WE, THEREFORE, SHOULD CONSIDER THE BANNING OF LANDMINES AS A STEP TOWARDS ULTIMATELY ACHIEVING GLOBAL DEMILITARISATION, FOR WHICH I AM DETERMINED TO DO WHATEVER I CAN.

AS A BUDDHIST MONK TO WHOM COMPASSION IS THE CORE PRACTICE, I ESPECIALLY ADMIRE THE NOBLE WORK OF THE INTERNATIONAL CAMPAIGN TO BAN LANDMINES. THE ETHICAL ASPECT OF COMPASSION IS TO REFRAIN FROM HARMING OTHERS - NOT JUST FELLOW HUMAN BEINGS BUT ALL LIVING BEINGS. THAT IS WHY IT IS IMPORTANT THAT WE TRY TO INCULCATE THE VALUE OF COMPASSION IN OUR HEARTS WHILE MAKING EFFORTS TO BAN DESTRUCTIVE WEAPONS, SUCH AS LANDMINES. *-H.H. Tenzin Gyatso, XIV Dalai Lama.*

HOLY GROUND

In the beginning when God created the heavens and the earth, the earth was a formless void and darkness covered the face of the deep, while a wind from God swept over the face of the waters

Genesis 1: 1-2

When the Lord saw that he had turned aside to see, God called to him out of the bush, 'Moses, Moses!' And he said, 'Here I am.' Then he said, 'Come no closer! Remove the sandals from your feet, for the place on which you are standing is holy ground.

Exodus 3:4-5

Then they came to Elim, where there were twelve springs of water and seventy palm trees; and they camped there by the water.

Exodus 15:27

He sustained him in a desert land, in a howling wilderness waste; he shielded him, cared for him, guarded him as the apple of his eye. As an eagle stirs up its nest, and hovers over its young; as it spreads its wings, takes them up, and bears them aloft on its pinions, the Lord alone guided him.

Deuteronomy 32: 10-12

...but those who wait for the Lord shall renew their strength, they shall mount up with wings like eagles, they shall run and not be weary. They shall walk and not faint.

Isaiah 40:31

For you shall go out in joy, and be led back in peace; the mountains and the hills before you shall burst into song, and all the trees of the field shall clap their hands.

Isaiah 55:12

DISARMAMENT HAS TAKEN IMPORTANT STEPS FORWARD WITH THE SIGNING OF THE TREATY COMPLETELY BANNING NUCLEAR TESTING ... THIS MUST NOT HOWEVER MAKE US LESS VIGILANT WITH REGARD TO THE PRODUCTION OF INCREASINGLY SOPHISTICATED CONVENTIONAL AND CHEMICAL WEAPONS, OR INDIFFERENT TO THE PROBLEMS CAUSED BY ANTI-PERSONNEL MINES.

- H.H. JOHN PAUL II, 13.1.1997

The service was arranged by The Peace Council, W 9643, Rucks Road, Cambridge, Wisconsin 53523 USA

A Selection of Anthologies

Appleton, George Ed. *The Oxford Book of Prayer,* OUP, 1985, Oxford.

> A substantial anthology of prayers of worship, petition, and intercession, personal and liturgical from Western, Eastern and Reformed Churches. Also prayers from the Jewish/Christian scriptures, and more than 100 pages of prayers from other traditions of faith.

Basset, Elizabeth *Love is My Meaning*: An Anthology of Assurance. Darton, Longman & Todd, 1973, London.

> A personal collection reflecting on and expressing the understandings of faith in a God of love which have proved helpful in 'sad times'. Mostly prose passages with some prayers and poetry. Mainly 19th and 20th century Western Christian.

Basset, Elizabeth *Interpreted by Love*: An Anthology of Praise. Darton, Longman & Todd, London, 1944.

> Praise of the Lord of all creation. Traditional Western Christian.

Boux, Dorothy. *The Golden Thread*: Words of Hope for a Changing World. Shepheard-Walwyn, London and Gateway Books, Bath, 1990.

> Spans many cultures and centuries with words of the wise about the journey from birth, through the wonders of creation to the revelation of that which underlies all life.

Butler, Donald G. Ed. *Many Lights.* Geoffrey Chapman, 1975

Clark, Susan J *Celebrating Earth Holy Days*: A Resource Guide for Faith Communities. Crossroad Publishing Co., 370 Lexington Avenue, New York, NY 10017, USA, 1992.

> Much practical environmental information, including liturgies, prayers, meditations - ancient and new - to celebrate the earth from a wide range of religious traditions, Jewish, Buddhist, Christian, Muslim, native American, African, and many more.

Deats, Richard Ed. *Ambassador of Reconciliation*: A Muriel Lester Reader. New Society Publishers, 4527 Springfield Avenue, Philadelphia PA 19143, USA, 1991.

> Muriel Lester's autobiography compiled from her writings. 'Pacifist, feminist and deeply spiritual ..... who practised what she preached. A close friend of Gandhi.' The book describes her work in London's East End, her resistance to both world wars, and her travels on behalf of the International Fellowship of Reconciliation.

Dinshaw, Nadir *A Wide-Open Heart*: An Interfaith Anthology of Christian Comment. Christian Action, St Peter's House, 308 Kennington Lane, London SE11 5HY, 1992.

> An anthology of widely ecumenical Christian prayers and reflections, mainly late 20th century.

Faivre, Daniel Ed. *Prayers of Hope of an Interfaith Man* (1989); *Creation*; *Transcendence* (1994); *Resources for Multifaith Celebrations*(1997). Westminster Interfaith
> Collections of religious texts from many faiths under topic headings with a comprehensive index.

Gollancz, Victor. *A Year of Grace*: Passages Chosen and Arranged to Express a Mood about God and Man. Penguin Books, UK, 1955.

> An anthology of praise and thanksgiving, predominantly Judaeo-Christian but including passages from classical writers and Hindu and Buddhist scriptures, philosophical and ethical in approach, substantial quotations several pages in length, also including short extracts, prayers and poetry.

Gollancz, Victor. *The New Year of Grace* Victor Gollancz Ltd, London, 1961.

> A clarification of the editor's conception of the idea of 'God and Man' with more incidental commentaries. An attempt to produce for youth and age an ordered account of one Man's religious and human philosophy, including much new material in a more easily assimilated form.

Greene, Barbara and Gollancz Victor, Eds. *God of a Hundred Names.* Victor Gollancz Ltd. London 1962.

> Poetry, hymns, prayers and short prose extracts designed as a source book for prayer and meditation by a Roman Catholic and self-described 'non-practising Judaeo-Christian' exploring the unity of intention observable behind seemingly disparate creeds.

Griffiths, Bede *Universal Wisdom*: A Journey Through the Sacred Wisdom of the World. Harper Collins Fount Press, 1994.

> 'An extraordinary collection of the world's great spiritual teachings from Hinduism, Buddhism, Taoism, Sikhism, Islam, Judaism, and Christianitry. Arranged in order of religious tradition, this ..... spiritual guide provides a ..... resource on the essence of the world's beliefs.'

Hayes, Will *The Stamper of the Skies*: A Bible for Animal Lovers. The Order of the Great Companions, 30 Montague St., London WC1, 1938.

> Holy Stories, prayers and poetry over the centuries from many cultures and traditions of faith celebrating the place of animals in creation.

Hayes, Will *Every Nation Kneeling* and Other Services of Prayer and Praise. Order of the Great Companions, Hertha's Chapel, Meopham Green, Kent, 1954.

> Fourteen services towards unity and peace from a Unitarian Church Minister.

Happold, F.C. *Mysticism*: A Study and an Anthology. Penguin Books, UK, 1963.

A study of Christian mysticism and an anthology of passages from writings of a few of the great mystics - Dionysius to Richard Jeffries - of sufficient length to give a more complete picture of their teachings than usually found in anthologies, including quotations from the Upanishads, the Bhagavad-Gita, Plato and the Sufis.

Hedges, Sid G. *Down to Earth and Up to Heaven*: Prayers for the Youthful. The Pilgrim Press, Robert Denholm House, Nutfield, Redhill, Surrey, 1964.

Prayers from a wide range of traditions adapted for Christian use, traditional in character.

Hedges, Sid G. *With One Voice*: Prayers and Thoughts from World Religions. The Religious Education Press, Ltd. Headington Hill Hall, Oxford, 1970.

Prayers in prose and poetry from a wide range of traditions with school assemblies in mind.

Humphrey, Nicholas, and Lifton, Robert Jay. Eds. *In a Dark Time*, Faber & Faber, London, 1984.

Poetry and prose from Sappho, Thucydides, St. John the Divine to the present day illustrating the insanity of war, finally giving hope that 'in a dark time the eye begins to see'. (Theodore Roethke).

Parrinder, Geoffrey. Collins *Dictionary of Religious and Spiritual Quotations*. Harper Collins, 1990 Hardback; 1992 Paperback.

Quotes from many religions topic by topic.

Prickett, John *Godspells* The Book Guild Ltd, Sussex, UK, 1992.

A collection of concise quotations with some comment, basically Christian, but including quotations from other faiths in the spirit of dialogue. 'An attempt to balance the religion of the heart, with the asceticism of the mind'.

Roberts, Elizabeth and Amidon, Elias. Eds. *Earth Prayers from Around the World*. Harper, 1991.

Satchidananda, Sri Swami *Lotus Prayer Book* Integral Yoga Publications, Route 1 Box 172, Buckingham, Virginia 23921, USA, 1986.

People from all faiths and cultures throughout history have envisioned and called to God in remarkably similar ways ..... A number of these themes ..... are illustrated with prayers from the ten major religions represented at LOTUS as well as from the lesser known faiths.'

Thompson, Denys. Ed. *Readings* Cambridge University Press 1974

A selection of passages from a wide and unorthodox range of sources arranged by themes of immediate and common concern.

Van de Weyer, Robert. *The Fount Book of Prayer* Harper Collins, London, 1993.

An erudite anthology of personal prayer from the Christian tradition over the centuries, with some texts from other traditions of faith, arranged alphabetically by author.

Whittaker, Agnes *All in the End is Harvest*: An Anthology for those who Grieve. Darton, Longman & Todd Ltd, London 1984.

Written in co-operation with the CRUSE organisation drawing both on great prose and poetry and also on good psychiatric literature which has proved helpful to bereaved people. Predominantly Western Christian 19th and 20th century.

Wilson, Andrew, Ed. *World Scripture*: A comparative Anthology of Sacred Texts. Paragon House, New York, 1991.

The shared beliefs of the world's religions, including Christianity, Judaism, Islam, Buddhism, Hinduism, Confucianism, Jainism, Sikhism, Baha'i Faith, Church of Jesus Christ of Latter-day Saints, and Zoroastrianism, and from the oral traditions of various primal religions world-wide.'

NOTES

Chapter 1 - Introduction

1. The British Red Cross Society Equal Opportunities Policy Statement of 15.7.91 (Ref: P 2/91: UK/BS/HV/SGA says of Religious Services:

    'It is fundamental to the Principles of the Red Cross that members of all faiths, and of none, are equally welcome. Also that the Society provides its services on an equally impartial basis. It is important that no official single faith Red Cross service should be initiated and held which could give rise to any other public perception. Where such services currently exist, Branches should seek alternative celebrations.

    Red Cross members, friends and and other officials should not, however, be discouraged from representing the Society at religious services of any faith, if invited to attend by other organisations: or from attending Remembrance services; or from organising events such as carol concerts for members of Red Cross clubs'.

Chapter 2
A History of the Development of Interfaith Services and the Discussion About Them

1 H. Barrows, *The World's Parliament of Religions*, p.67.

2 Ibid, p.155 and p.186.

3 M.K. Gandhi, *Ashram Observances in Action*, Navajivan Publication, Ahmedabad 1955, p.23.

4 Will Hayes, *Every Nation Kneeling*, The Order of the Great Companions, Meopham Green, Kent, 1954.

5 Resolution of British Council of Churches at the 1968 Spring meeting, quoted in *Inter-Faith Worship*, Ed Marcus Braybrooke, Galliard/Stainer and Bell 1974, p.5.

6 Report to BCC, quoted *Inter-Faith Worship*, pp. 5-6.

7 *Interfaith Worship*, Ed Marcus Braybrooke. See note 5

8 Peter R Akenhurst and R W F Wootton, *Interfaith Worship?* Grove Booklet No 52, Bramcote, Notts. 1977.

9 *Ends and Odds*, Newsletter Ed by Peter Schneider, No.22, March 1980.

10 *Can We Pray Together?*, Committee for Relations with People of Other Faiths, British Council of Churches, 1983.

11 David Bookless, *Interfaith Worship and Christian Truth*, Grove Worship Booklet No 117, Bramcote, Notts, 1991.

12 *Multi-Faith Worship?* Church House Publishing, 1992 .

13 *The Marriage of Adherents of Other Faiths in Anglican Churches*, Board of Mission Occasional Paper 1, 1992 and *Guidelines for the Celebration of Mixed-Faith Marriages in Church,* Board of Mission Occasional Paper No 2., 1992.

14 'Multi-faith Worship'? Guidance on the Situations which arise. GS Misc. 411. Church House Bookshop, 1993.

15 'The Open Letter' was produced by the 'Open Letter Group', PO Box 448, London SW19 6SD. The letter asking clergy to sign the letter is dated 20.9.91.

16 *The Times,* 1.10.91 and *The Bath Chronicle* Oct 1991.

17 Brother Daniel Le Faivre, *Creation*, Westminster Interfaith Programme, *Prayer of Hope of an Interfaith Man*. BFSS National RE Centre, 1989 and *Resources for Multifaith Celebrations,* Westminster Interfaith 1997.

18 For example, the Methodist Church and the United Reform Church.

19   See for example the devotional services arranged for Sarva Dharma Sammelana in Bangalore in 1993, which are reproduced in *Visions of an Interfaith Future*, Ed Celia and David Storey, International Interfaith Centre, Oxford OX1 3EF, 1994 or *Assembly of the World's Religions 1990*, Ed Thomas G Walsh, A New Era Book, International Religious Foundation, Inc, New York 1992.

20   See *Sharing Worship, Communicatio in Sacris,* Ed Paul Puthanangady, National Biblical Catechetical and Liturgical Centre, Bangalore 560 084, India, 1988.

21   *In Prayer for Peace,* the record of the Day of Prayer for World Peace, 27.10.86, p.23.

22   Cardinal Roger Etchegaray, *Ibid,* pp.20-21

23   *Religion and Nature Interfaith Ceremony,* WWF 25th Anniversary, 29.9.86 Programme.

24   *The Times*, 11.12.91, p.20

25   *Sharing Worship, op cit.,* p.47

26   *Ibid,* p.49

27   *Ibid*, pp. 55-6

28   *Ibid*, p.87

29   *Ibid*, p.88

30   *Ibid*, p.789

31   *Ibid*, p.791

32   *Ibid*, p.463

33   *Ibid*, pp. 459-481

34   *Ibid*, p. 800

35   *Ibid*, pp. 59-62

36   *Ibid,* p.587

37   *Ibid*, p.595

38   *Ibid*, pp. 659-667

39   *Ibid*, p.67

40   *Clifford's Tower Commemoration,* B'nai B'rith Jewish Music Festival and CCJ 1990, pp.92-3

41   Quoted in *L'Elyah*, London, Spring 1987.

42   Unpublished report of a meeting of The Inter Faith Network for the UK on 'Inter Faith Worship and Prayer: The Current Controversy', 16.1.1992.   Quotations are used with permission.

43   *The Times,* 18.12.91

44   See *Gemeinsame Christlich-judische Gottesdientse?   Analyse - Grundfragen - Vorschlage.*   Ed Arnulf Baumann, Ulrich Schwemer, Veld/Klak, quoted by Hans Ucko in *Current Dialogue* 24, WCC (see note 48).

45   See further Judy Petsonk and Jim Remsen *The Intermarriage Handbook* Quill, William Morrow 1988 and Jonathan A Romain, *Till Faith Us Do Part,* Fount (Harper/Collins), 1996.

46   Marcia Littell, *Liturgies on the Holocaust,* The Edwin Mellen Press, Lewiston N.Y and Queenston, Ontario, 1986, p.7.

47   Report of a Plenary Meeting of the Inter Faith for the UK on 'Inter Faith Worship and Prayer: The Current Controversy', 16.1.1992.

48   'Inter-Religious Worship and Prayer' by Hans Ucko in *Current Dialogue* 24, June 1993, World Council of Churches, Geneva, pp. 35-9.

49   'Report on Inquiry on Interreligious Prayer and Worship' by Hans Ucko in *Current Dialogue* 28, June 1995, World Council of Churchs, Geneva, pp. 57-64.

50   The Statement and papers of the Bangalore 1996 consultation on interreligious prayer. See also my article in *The Tablet* for 26.7.96.

51   'Guidelines for Interfaith Celebration and Worship' of the American Presbyterian Church Task group.   Draft 6/3/96.

Chapter 3 - The Issues

1 Will Hayes, *Every Nation Kneeling,*op. cit., p.7.
2 Francis Younghusband in *Religions of Empire,* ed William Loftus Hare, pp.18-9.
3 Archbishop George Appleton, Sermon at WCF Service at King's College Chapel, London, in June 1972, quoted in *Inter-Faith Worship,* p.8.
4 Swami Tripurananda in a paper to the WCF Ammerdown Conference, November 1994. He quoted from Swami Vivekananda's *My Master,* New York 1895.
5 See below p.34.
6 Quoted from *Ends and Odds,* op cit., Para 6.7
7 H Montefiore, Sermon at Great St Mary's, Cambridge 24.9.67, quoted in *Inter-Faith Worship,* p.8.
8 *Church Times* 12.1.90.   See also replies in the *Church Times,* 19.1.90 and *Interfaith Update,* published by The Open Letter Group, London, n.d.
9 Quoted by Hans Küng in *Global Ethic,* SCM Press 1993, p.64.
10 See below, p.36.
11 See for a useful introduction, Alan Race, *Christians and Religious Pluralism,* SPCK, 1983 and 1993.
12 See for a fuller discussion, Marcus Braybrooke, *Faith in a Global Age,* Braybrooke Press 1995
13 An Observance for Commonwealth Day, 1997.
14. *Sharing Worship, op cit.,* pp.597-604.

Chapter 7
Hindu Worship and Prayer in the Context of Inter-Faith Worship

1 Ranchor Prime adds 'I speak from the Vaishnava tradition of the Bhagavad Gita. The majority of Hindus in Great Britain come from Vaishnava families, though I believe my words will also apply to other Hindu traditions'.

Chapter 11 - Interfaith Co-operation -
A Matter of Faith for Sikhs

1 This article, in abbreviated form, is based on an address to the World's Parliament of Religions in Chicago in 1993.

Chapter 13 - Universal Worship

1 This passage is an extract from a talk on Worship by Swami Vivekananda at the 1893 World's Parliament of Religions.   It was quoted by Swami Tripulananda of The Ramakrishan Vedanta Society of the World Congress of Faiths Conference on Interfaith Prayer at Ammerdown, near Bath in 1994.

Chapter 14 - Local Initiatives

Much of this Chapter was written as a result of the questionnaires sent to Inter-Faith Groups - see Acknowledgments.

Chapter 33
The Opening Ceremony of Our British Interfaith Ecological Centre

1   Sarva-Dharma-Sammelana: *Religious People Meeting Together* used during the opening ceremony of an Interfaith meeting at Bangalore, India, 19-22 August 1993.

2   These may be substituted depending on availability.

3   Palmer, Martin, Nash, Anne & Hattingh, Ivan, *Faith and Nature*, London: Century Hutchinson Ltd (WWF), 1987, p.7

4   Nhat Hahn Thich, 'Earth Gathas' in *Dharma Gaia*, Ed. Allan Hunt Badiner. Berkeley: Parallax Press: 1990. p.195-7

5   This information is taken from an interview with a Hindu lady in Leicester with her kind permission.

6   Quoted in Palmer, *op.cit.,* p.46

7   'S' is an abbreviated form of the phrase 'Peace be on him' or 'May Allah bless him and grant him peace' which is said by Muslims in Arabic as a sign of respect.

8   Schimmel, Annemarie, 'The Celestial Garden in Islam'. In *The Islamic Garden*. Ed. Richard Ettinghausen. Washington: Dumbarton Oaks: 1976, 11.

9   Philip Pick, Tu Bi Shevat: A happy New Year to all Trees, in *Judaism & Ecology,* Ed. Aubrey Rose, Cassell, London, 1992, 69.

10   Quoted in Holm, Jean & Barker, John *Attitudes to Nature*, Pinto, London, pp.132-147.

11   Halifax, Joan, 'The Third Body' in *Dharma Gaia,* Ed Allan Hunt Badiner, Berkeley: Parallax Press, 1990 pp 20-38.

CONTRIBUTORS

Shahin Bekhradnia, Zoroastrian

Rev. Marcus Braybrooke, Chair, World Congress of Faiths.

Claire Dalley, former student of Westminster College, Oxford.

Hilary Freeman, Member of the Baha'i Assembly of Tandridge

Vinod Kapashi, Jain

Rabbi Rachel Montagu, Member of the Council of Reform and Liberal Rabbis

Rev. John Pridmore, Rector of Hackney

Mrs Jean Potter, Community Relations Adviser to the UK Girl Guides Association, 1972-1982

Ranchor Prime, a Vaishnavite Hindu

Dr Abduljalil Sajid, Director Brighton Islamic Centre and Mosque

Ranbir Singh Sandhu, Sikh

Ven. Pandith M. Vajiragnana, Sangha Navaka of Great Britain.

© The Editors are grateful to all who have given permission to include copyright material. especially Stainer and Bell Ltd, London, England, David Higham Associates, Essex Music Group, Jubilate Hymns, Richard Boeke and The Week of Prayer for World Peace.

ACKNOWLEDGMENTS

The Editors would like to thank all who have given their advice and made suggestions concerning the Anthology.   These include :

Hugh Adamson, Sakina Daudjee, Rev. Jonathan Gorsky, Sandy Martin, Swami Siva Nandhi, Brian Pearce, Rev. Alan Race, Saba Risaluddin, Rabbi Jonathan Romain, Charanjit Ajit Singh, Dr. Gur-Dave Singh, Indarjit Singh, Ajahn Sunnato, Rev. Dr. Robert Traer, Swami Tripurananda, Rev. Frank Whaling, and all those who participated in the Ammerdown Conference in 1994.

Also Stella Clarke, Dick Richmond and Richard Westgarth for valuable help with graphics.

The Editors would also like to thank the following who returned questionnaires with very helpful comments and suggestions :

Ramona Kauth	Birmingham Interfaiths Council
Molly Kenyon	Bradford Concord Interfaith Society
Anula Beckett & June Ridd	Bristol Inter-Faith Group
Rev. Jean Clark	Coventry Inter-Faith Group
Canon David Tann	Dudley Council of Faiths
Sandy Martin	Exeter Interfaith Society
Rosemary Eldridge	Glasgow Sharing of Faiths
Arnie Gabbott	Hammersmith & West London College of Further Education
Martin Palmer	International Consultancy on Religion, Education and Culture
Rabbi Jonathan Romain	Maidenhead Community Consultative Committee
Marian Liebmann	Mediation U.K.
Joyce Howell	Redbridge Council of Faiths
Edwin Smith	West Bromwich Interfaith Forum
Fr. Michael Barnes	Westminster Interfaith
Brian Reep	Woking Interfaith Group
Ivy Gutridge	Wolverhampton Inter-Faith Group
Jennifer Beresford	Wycombe Sharing of Faiths
Mary Hayward	York College Religious Education Centre

WORLD CONGRESS OF FAITHS

Registered Charity 244096

The World Congress of Faiths (WCF) was founded in 1936 by Sir Francis Younghusband. In 1903, in Lhasa, Tibet, he had a decisive spiritual experience of an underlying unity of all beings. His hope was that, through WCF, members of all religious traditions would become aware of this universal experience and that 'the roots of fellowship would strike down deep to the Central Source of all spiritual loveliness'. The WCF, which is based in Britain, has arranged a wide variety of conferences, helping people to learn about other faiths and to rethink traditional attitudes of opposition and hostility. It has encouraged members to appreciate one another's spiritual practices and on occasions to pray together. WCF has developed links with like-minded groups across the world and has helped to establish the International Interfaith Centre at Oxford. Its journal, *World Faiths Encounter,* which is supplied free to members, is an important forum for discussion of interfaith concerns and developments. Marcus Braybrooke's *A Wider Vision*, published by Oneworld Publications, tells the history of the movement. Anyone sympathetic to the ideals of the World Congress of Faiths is welcome to apply for membership, which costs £20.

WORLD CONGRESS OF FAITHS
2 Market Street
Oxford OX1 3EF